*Unlearning the Basics*

# Unlearning the Basics

*A New Way of Understanding Yourself and the World*

Rishi Sativihari

Foreword by Mu Soeng

Wisdom Publications ◆ Boston

Wisdom Publications
199 Elm Street
Somerville MA 02144 USA
www.wisdompubs.org

*Library of Congress Cataloging-in-Publication Data*
Sativihari, Rishi.
 Unlearning the basics : a new approach to the Four Noble Truths / Rishi Sativi-hari ; foreword by Mu Soeng.
  p. cm.
Includes bibliographical references and index.
ISBN 0-86171-572-1 (pbk. : alk. paper)
1. Four Noble Truths. I. Title.
BQ4230.S28 2010
294.3'42—dc22
                                        2010007995

14 13 12 11 10
5  4  3  2  1

Cover design by JBTL. Interior design by Gopa & Ted2, Inc.
Set in Guardi LT 10.25/16.3.

*Dedication*

This study is dedicated to four of my teachers: to Venerable Wattegama Dhammawasa Mahathero, who offered me a spiritual home and showed me the meaning of a consecrated life; to Venerable Peradeniye Sujatha Thero, who shared the heart of the Dharma with me and encouraged me to help Westerners hear its beat; to Bernard Lonergan, S.J. (1904–1984), who taught me to notice and appreciate the subtleties of the Western mind; and to Dr. Otto Weininger (1929–2005), who taught me to listen compassionately to children until I could hear the wisdom hidden in their fantasies.

# Contents

# Foreword

It is axiomatic that the teachings of the Buddha have found their integrity and authenticity in each generation in the lives as well as interpretative efforts of a handful of practitioners and thinkers. At no time have these interpretations been more visible or thoughtful (or numerous) as we have seen in the West in the last twenty or thirty years. This is the first time in the history of this 2,500-year-old tradition that all various major and secondary schools have come together under a single roof, so to speak. The religious pluralism of North America, in conjunction with a number of other historical factors, has shaped the landscape of Buddha's teachings on these shores like no other time in history. Accordingly, Buddhist practitioners and thinkers have been forced to compete in a marketplace of ideas, to work in a more demanding and more sophisticated environment than the simple ethos of Buddhist missionaries and preachers in ancient and medieval Asian societies. These teachers have had to deal with the impact of modernity on Buddha's teachings and have had to find their own new voice in negotiating an unexpectedly new terrain.

Rishi Sativihari's is one of these new voices and it's a pleasure to sit back and listen to it. His book remains focused on the Four

Noble Truths and his interpretation of these truths in the light of our contemporary understanding of psychological and biological processes is a rewarding experience. He makes the historically correct argument that, in all his forty-five years of teaching ministry, the Buddha himself remained focused on the Four Noble Truths. Anything he said in those forty-five years was but a variation on the first sermon he ever gave, the Dhammacakkapavatana Sutta in Pali (Turning the Wheel of Dharma), after his great awakening experience. To come back to the contents of that first sermon is to recover the authenticity of that awakening experience as well as the integrity of its expression. Sativihari's argument that "the four truths were given in a certain order, not only for the sake of creating a logical system of thought, but because experientially they emerged in that way in the Buddha's life, building progressively on one another" never rang more true.

If there is any "system" at all in the Buddha's teachings, the Four Noble Truths are that system. These truths (or reflections, if you will) are secular, etiological, and universally human. They are free of the ontological promiscuities and speculative metaphysics in which so many religious systems get bogged down. *Unlearning the Basics* remains impeccably faithful to these orientations of the Four Noble Truths and this orientation is what makes his book an exciting read.

This book is in many ways a model for how the teachings of the Buddha could and should be talked about in a psychologically mature and sophisticated manner, in a way congruent with recent findings in brain research and cognitive science. Sativihari touches upon these researches and findings to supplement his own innovative insights into what the Buddha was trying to convey to his audience in his explication of the Four Noble Truths. Sativihari's commitment to using Pali and Sanskrit words as his primary frame of reference, rather than their often garbled and confusing English translations, lend a much-appreciated gravitas to his presentation.

This is an important book and I hope it gets the wide audience it deserves. It adds much to the current discourses and also brings us much closer to a more nuanced understanding of the Buddha's own thought processes.

Mu Soeng
Barre, Massachusetts

Mu Soeng is the scholar-in-residence at the Barre Center for Buddhist Studies, and is the author of three books exploring seminal Buddhist texts: *Heart of the Universe: Exploring the Heart Sutra; The Diamond Sutra: Transforming the Way We See the World;* and *Trust in Mind: The Rebellion of Chinese Zen.*

# Preface

The language of Dharma conveys a sense of spiritual truth—
that relates fundamentally to the art of living. To be real Dharma
language, it must thus contain wisdom regarding the nature of
this human life, its promise and its predicaments, and how that
human life may best be lived. In this way, Dharma is akin to both
philosophy and religion in the deepest sense of these words—in
terms of "loving wisdom" (the etymological root of *philosophy*)
and "reconnecting" to a greater whole (the root of *religion*).
Dharma asks key questions about life and suggests answers to
those questions.

When the Buddha began teaching his Dharma in India two
and a half millennia ago, he taught it in a simple four-part form
that came to be called the Four Noble Truths. In his forty years of
teaching, he expressed these same essential truths in a variety of
ways and a variety of contexts. When the word *Dharma* is used in
the Buddhist context, it refers primarily to the body of teachings
that has evolved around the core of these four truths.

But what actually are the four truths? What is their nature? In
an important way, in the four truths, the Buddha is essentially
communicating *himself* to us. He is describing his own spiritual

quest: the journey of his life and the path that he followed to liberation. From the process of describing his own quest, a comprehensive philosophy of life unfolds; and the Buddha goes on to teach truths grounded in his personal experience yet also embedded in the very nature of reality.

In another way, we can look at the four truths as a kind of sacred poem. Indeed, this poetic sense of the four truths at the heart of their wisdom remains as yet in important ways largely unexplored in the West, where we are instead more focused on technical philosophical and psychological interpretations of the Buddhadharma. In my own experience hearing Buddhist sermons in Sanskrit-based languages, they often have a power that is not paralleled in English Buddhist talks. And that power is the power of poetry. The poetic vision at the core of the four truths opens the minds of listeners to the person of the Buddha and to his vision of the spiritual quest as both transcendent and profoundly human. This poetic apprehension requires us to feel the living heart that is still beating within these truths and to find ways to give voice to what that heart—and indeed our heart—is saying now.

My aim in this volume is an imperfect effort to move in that direction. I aim at telling the story of the four truths—the story of the Buddha's spiritual quest—using images and metaphors that are, I hope, accessible and resonant to the poetic imaginations of the reader. In the telling of the story, Buddhist philosophy and psychology are woven in, as reflection and commentary, around the poetic core of the four truths.

In so doing, I will necessarily be taking a certain amount of poetic license, even as I try to hew closely to the essence of the teachings. As I present my own views and interpretations, the best I can do is put forward what I have tested in my own life and found to be true, what I have found to be helpful in my own quest for greater virtue, self-awareness, and wisdom. And of course, my hope is that when readers test it in their own lives, they will also find something of real value.

The four truths can be summed up each by a Pali word: *dukkha, tanha, nirodha,* and *magga.* These words translate roughly as "suffering," "thirst," "cessation," and "path"—but any single-word English translation is, I feel, inadequate. For this reason, I will be using the Pali throughout this work. Four of the first five chapters of this volume are devoted to exploration in depth of one of these four truths and these four terms.

The Buddha presented the four truths in a certain order, not only for the sake of creating a coherent system of thought, but because experientially they emerged in that order in the Buddha's life, building progressively on one another. Understand the truth of dukkha well, and you will find the illusions of tanha at its core. See into the illusions of tanha, and you will discover the mystery of nirodha. Once enveloped by that mystery, even if only for a moment, you will have a clear grasp of the entire journey of life, as the Buddha experienced it and as you too can experience it. When you understand the journey described in the first three truths, if that understanding indeed resonates with your own experience of your journey, you will see your need for refuge, and embrace the pragmatic path that will guide you through the intricacies of this journey in your everyday life.

Yet the description of the path really only makes sense in relation to the journey itself, just as a map only makes sense when we actually understand the geography of where we are and where it is that we are intending to explore. Indeed, if we don't ground our understanding of the path in our own journey, these teachings can become a source of frustration or confusion.

The Buddha's Path is not a neutral technology. It won't, like some magic carpet, just take us *anywhere* we want to go. Its end is a virtuous life, grounded in self-awareness and wisdom. There are various obstacles to this end that we must attend to along the way. As a result, not all of the places that the path takes us to are pleasant. So before wandering too far down the path, we are wise to be fairly clear about the nature of the journey, which the path serves.

The teachings in this book honor each and every person who contributed time, space, love, and support to the development of the Contemplative Living group, a small community of about fifteen persons who have met together every week over the past five years to explore ways to live their lives with greater virtue, self-awareness, and wisdom. The teachings of the Buddha have been the group's common spiritual framework, although members have a variety of religious backgrounds, including Buddhist, Jewish, Christian (Catholic and Protestant), Muslim, and atheist. This primer was developed over the years in the context of the group's ongoing practice and conversations. The love, struggles, and commitment of each person in the group helped inspire and refine every page. Any problems with the text, however, are the sole responsibility of the author.

# CHAPTER ONE

# Introduction

## *What Is the Mind?*

Every culture has its own myths or traditional stories about what mind is. One of the common stories in our culture is that mind is a "faculty of thought." On account of this story, we tend to associate mind with a person's intellect and memory, and perhaps with that person's emotions, what we call the will and even the personality. And, when pressed, most people in our culture will imagine the mind as being located in the head region.

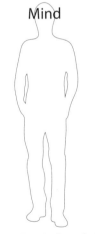

*Our culture's view of mind*

Mind in the time of the Buddha was imagined quite differently. It described a more holistic, integrated consciousness. It was understood as being something like an invisible thread that interconnects all of our bodily sensations, thoughts, emotions, and so on. It was the unified whole of consciousness, not just a piece of it, such as "intellect" or "belief" or "body" or "feeling." The mind was thus in your *knee* just as much as it was in your head. And it was in matter itself, in form, not simply "over" it or epiphenomenal to it. It was regarded as a kind of stream that flows through all domains of a person, revealing them to be one whole; or, alternatively, like a braided cord, weaving these domains together. Thus, in the Buddhist view, mind entirely fills the body.

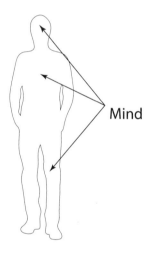

*The Buddhist view of mind*

For this reason, sometimes the ancient Indian words in the Pali/Sanskrit language for mind (*mano* or *chitta*) are translated into English as "heart"—because in our Western cultural stories, the word "heart" often has more of a sense of integration. It is, in short, less confined to the head region. It should also be noted that, related to this, some East Asian languages do not distinguish between "mind" and "heart" linguistically.

Mind in ancient India also extended across space and time: mind was manifest, for example, in physical movements and speech acts. Such acts could be seen as actually *containing* mind, not simply as the *products of* a mind located elsewhere.

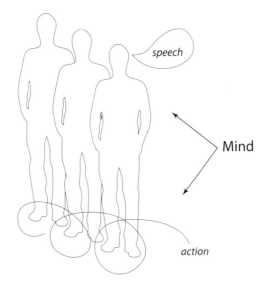

*Mind is also embodied in words and action.*

Another dimension of the constantly flowing mind that we find in the stories of ancient India is that it did not just stop streaming at the boundary of the individual body, or even at its physical and verbal expressions. Rather, the mind's extension of itself was in fact *universal* in scope. To illustrate this conception of the mind, the universe is pictured below (on a very small scale!), with "mind" as a stream or thread, running through all that is. In this view, mind sustains "my" individual consciousness, and also extends *beyond* my individual consciousness into your individual consciousness, and those of other sentient beings, and the rest of the universe as well. But it isn't limited even to all beings and things, sentient and nonsentient, that exist; it extends beyond *everything*, beyond space, and beyond time—beyond "existence" itself.

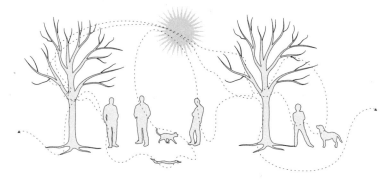

*The thread of mind extends throughout the whole of the universe.*

This ancient Indian story of mind is clearly a very different story than Western culture is accustomed to. The Buddha did not explicitly teach this view, but it can nonetheless be seen or inferred at places in his teachings. Indeed, for the people to whom the Buddha was teaching, this story of mind would have been central to how they interpreted his teachings.

An important thing to consider about such a myth of the mind is that it does *not* suggest, as is often expressed, "we are all one." Rather, what it suggests is that there is *both* separateness and interrelatedness. And what's more, our inability to perceive and honor this both-separateness-and-interrelatedness is an underlying theme in many of our problems—psychologically, socially, politically, and environmentally. It may be that this ancient story about the nature of the mind—which is so very different from our own individualist and intellectualist stories—deserves more attention.

## Levels of Consciousness

In the Buddha's teachings, the mind is imagined as having various "levels." At the most gross level, the mind's consciousness of itself is very limited. As a result, perception at this level is very individualistic, pertaining to "me" and "mine." Indeed, at the grossest level, mind may even regard certain aspects *of itself* as unwelcome, intrusive, or foreign. At the gross level of awareness, there are thick and impermeable boundaries perceived around the individual person's body. And everything outside of that boundary is (erroneously) understood by the gross mind in terms of this very limited, individualistic consciousness. In contrast, at the most subtle level, the mind's consciousness is beyond individuality, space, and time, and is impossible to describe in words. In between the most gross and the most subtle levels, the mind is aware, in varying degrees, of its interconnectedness to all of life. Thus mind (at least at its deepest levels) is not a closed individual system that only operates inside of our skin or our own head, as we often imagine it to be. Rather, it is a pervasive quality of the universe.

How "true" something is, in this view, depends primarily on the nature of the mind doing the perceiving. A person can say, "I see that cat." But what that actually means even to the person saying it depends on the relative clarity of that person's mind. When the mind is functioning only at the most gross level of consciousness, it is very "egocentric." It perceives things, but it perceives them as separate parts of a universe in which it is the center. The boundaries between self and other are not porous; it is as though the otherwise-permeable boundaries have become clogged up, as sometimes happens with air filters, preventing the free flow of air.

As the quality of mind is refined through meditation and the Buddhist Path, however, the perception of interconnectedness-amid-separateness deepens and, because of that, true compassion—caring for Other as we do for Self—deepens as well. When this happens, Other is present and integrated within my very perception of myself and awareness is no longer confined to a narcissistic or solipsistic circle. When we hear Buddhist texts speaking of "a heart that holds the whole world," we may imagine this describes some kind of incredible emotional superhero. But in fact, it is simply a poetic way of referring to this more subtle and refined level of consciousness, beyond the confines of the self-important circle.

But understanding or believing this and seeing it for ourselves are two different things. We can *understand* the concept that the mind has very subtle levels in which everything that exists is interconnected. We can even *believe* that this concept is true, and even value it highly, trying to base our actions on it. And indeed this belief can produce wonderful consequences. The world may become a better place as a result of such beliefs and actions. But this does not mean that we are actually conscious of the subtle nature of the mind. It does not mean that we actually perceive those interconnections to others in the present moment. This distinction is very important. Deepening and refining one's level of consciousness is not simply a matter of holding the right metaphysical beliefs; it is a matter of perceptual clarity.

We can see how easy it would be to slip into misunderstandings of the Buddha's teachings when we try to make sense of them with the concepts of the "mind" that arise from the myths of our own contemporary culture. To illustrate the importance of this, consider the following small text from the Dhammapada, one of the earliest and most succinct presentations of the Dharma:

Mind is the forerunner of all things.
If a person speaks and acts
with a mind that is impure,
then suffering follows her,
like the wheel that follows the foot of an ox.

If a person speaks and acts
with a mind that is pure,
then flourishing follows her,
just like her never-departing shadow.

Notice how differently this could be interpreted, depending on how one understands the word "mind." If we have a restricted, intellectualist understanding of "mind," we might come away from this quote understanding that the Buddha's Dharma is essentially just a technology of "positive thinking." But the meaning changes and broadens dramatically when we consider this from the perspective of mind as pervading and interconnecting.

## Obscurations

One important metaphor that the Buddha used in his teaching to describe how awareness of the mind becomes obscured was the process of dust piling up on the surface of an object. The dust is inevitable illusions or delusions that arise in consciousness about the nature of oneself and the world. These are what produce *kile-shas,* sometimes translated as "defilements" or "obscurations," the harmful qualities of greed, hatred, and purposeful ignorance. Although the mind is by nature clear, we become unable to see into its more subtle depths because of all of the dust that collects on its surface.

The first question that the Buddha's Dharma asks and answers is about what we would see if this dust were to be somehow swept away and we were to look clearly into the subtle depths of the mind. We would experience the mind in its natural state, undistorted by illusion. The Buddha taught that, from his experience, this natural state is recognizable by certain signs, among which are the following:

- an unusual quality of happiness, which is deeper than, and can be felt in spite of, the inevitable ups and downs, pleasures and pains, of life.
- self-awareness.
- open self-expression, without concealed intentions.
- caring about the well-being of self and others.
- generosity.
- awareness and honoring of the boundaries between self and others.
- treasuring and protecting of the mind's awareness of itself.
- the ability—called *wisdom*—to see deeply into the nature of the human predicament, to understand its causes and solutions.

The mind in which clarity has been obscured is also recognizable by certain signs, among which are these:

- an unusual quality of suffering, which is deeper than, and permeates, the inevitable ups and downs, pleasures and pains, of life. It is a suffering that reflects the failure to perceive human potential.

+ a lack of self-awareness.
+ concealment of intentions.
+ a lack of caring about the well-being of self and others.
+ unwillingness to give and share.
+ lack of awareness of or dishonoring of the boundaries between self and others.
+ treasuring and protecting of unawareness.
+ an inability to see the nature of the human predicament, its causes and solutions.

The next question that the Buddha's Dharma asks and answers has to do with the conditions that lead to the build-up of obscurations. What causes the obscuration of the mind in its natural state? The Buddha spoke of five main conditions, under which the clarity of the mind becomes obscured. They suggest that bodily well-being is essential to the clarity of the mind. The five baseline necessities for the development of clarity are these:

+ adequate nutrition.
+ adequate shelter.
+ adequate clothing.
+ adequate medicine.
+ adequate spiritual community.

The first four conditions have to do with physical deprivation (and here it should be noted that, regarding the fourth, "adequate medicine" would have included the physical yoga, lifestyle prescriptions, and perhaps even dietary supplements necessary to maintain a healthy body). The fifth condition is more complex. It points to the lack of a *sangha*, a Pali word meaning "spiritual community," as a condition out of which mental obscuration arises. A healthy sangha is a community of people in which there is understanding, embodiment, and teaching of good dharma. In this sense, the lowercased word *dharma* refers to a worldview that asks key questions about life and suggests answers to those questions. It is not simply a philosophical system, or a certain kind of lifestyle. All communities of people embody a dharma of one sort or another, and this dharma reflects the shared stories and values of the community. The Buddha's Dharma is also fundamentally oriented toward liberation—toward the resolution of suffering and the promotion of flourishing. And, in this sense, a "good" dharma is one that subjectively *works*—one that actually promotes the happiness associated with human flourishing, and actually diminishes the suffering associated with failing to realize human potential. Thus, this fifth condition is quite a stiff requirement!

It means that in order for a human being to fully flourish, he or she requires free access to a community of people that understand, embody, and teach the art of living. It suggests that the Buddha's Dharma is thus not simply a matter of ideas, but that its truths are experiential and relational in nature. The Dharma is embedded within a community of people. Therefore, if my interactions are restricted to a community of people who do not value or encourage the flourishing of all of its members, I am in a social context that will make it extraordinarily difficult for me to learn the dharmic art of living. On the other hand, even in very dismal contexts, if there are even one or two persons who can affirm and support my potential as a human being, spiritual community can develop and remarkable growth and evolution can occur.

Emphasizing the importance of community, the Buddha taught his followers that if they should find themselves in a superior spiritual community, one which facilitates the development of their minds, but the other four requisites are not that reliable, they should nonetheless hang in there with that community as best they can. Such a community is priceless, the Buddha said, and their virtue will most likely lead to an improvement of the material conditions. On the other hand, if they were to find themselves in an inferior spiritual community where their mental development is difficult to sustain, even if the four physical requisites are present better than they have ever had before, they should nonetheless pack up and leave that very night.

For the Buddha, to expect that any person could get very far on the path to inner peace, compassion, and wisdom without the nourishing influence of a healthy spiritual community was absurd. It would be like expecting to enjoy vibrant physical health in the absence of food, shelter, clothing, and healthcare. What this suggests is that we require friends, in the deepest sense of the word: other human beings who care about us and our ultimate well-being, in addition to caring about their own journey. Such people are sometimes found in formally spiritual places, such as temples, mosques, churches, and meditation groups. Sometimes they are discovered at work, or in our neighborhood. Sometimes we are fortunate enough to have such people within our own biological family. But we must find such people—and wherever we find them, we must make sure that we experience their influence on our lives on a regular basis.

Cultivating such an experience of spiritual community takes time. Rather than being something that we can just go shopping for, it is more like something that we have to, at least in part, grow within ourselves. Often it is through a process of extending ourselves, and becoming such a friend to others, that we become more aware of the presence of people who are doing the same thing, as well as of those who clearly are not, and in this way we end up discovering, attracting, and being attracted to our own supportive spiritual community.

It is often said that difficult experiences "build character." From the Buddha's perspective, there is certainly truth in that statement—but the character that they help to build is not always a healthy or a virtuous one! Difficult experiences can also foster highly destructive qualities of character. A great deal depends on our context. Having the five requisites in place, especially the availability of a healthy spiritual community, seems to be the key to making good use of difficulty. Such resources provide us with the physical, social, and emotional support—and the deeper spiritual guidance—that we need to clearly understand what is happening and how best to respond to it. This seems to make all the difference. If we faced exactly the same difficulties in a physically impoverished context, without wise and supportive role models, the challenges we experienced would be immeasurably greater, and a beneficial outcome far less likely. Having a good context seems to be everything, especially in the early phases of spiritual development. It needs to be assured before undertaking the spiritual quest. This is just one of the built-in limitations of our nature as interdependent beings.

## The Contemplative Life

Another quality that community supports is contemplative living, which in the Buddhist perspective is a way of life that engages the person as a whole. Although it is very clearly focused on the life of the mind, it understands mind in a profoundly holistic way. And so, it engages the intellectual life, the emotional life, and the social/relational life, as well as that mystery of life that transcends all such categorizations. Contemplative living seeks to engage these various dimensions of life in an integrated and integrating fashion.

If we become true contemplatives, we become people who are concerned with expanding our mind's horizon, so that we can understand ourselves and others, and life itself, as much and as deeply as is possible. We strive to understand these essentials in the heart, in the intellect, in action, in a thoroughly embodied way. We do this because, to some extent, we have already become aware that it is only this sort of knowledge that will allow us, and those around us, to flourish as human beings. To flourish as a human being is something deeper than having everything go our way in life. Flourishing in this true sense is a process that can continue, through good times and bad, even through the most painful realities of life.

Engendering this flourishing is the primary goal of the Buddhist Sangha. The Buddha himself, though, was not primarily interested in developing a new religion. Rather, his orientation was what we might now call interfaith or multi-faith. He did not want to draw people out of their various religious homes. Rather, he hoped that people would learn his Dharma—his spiritual teachings on the art of living—bring them back into their own religious contexts, and use them there to enhance their lives. Because of this intention, the original Indian teachings were minimalist and, in a certain way, universal. They contained very few rites, rituals, or metaphysical beliefs.

It was also the Buddha's conviction that the Dharma, which he had come to understand, and the contemplative life that it encouraged, was not unique to him. He did not invent it. Rather, it reflected truths that had always been understood by wise persons of all eras, all religions, philosophies, genders, races, and classes. If we were to express his approach in the language of contemporary society, we might say that his teachings were truly ecumenical, to be explored by people of all faiths, not for the sake of converting them, but to help them be better Christians, more enlightened Muslims, more integrated Hindus, Jews, existentialists, atheists, and so on. The borders of contemplative life are wide open to all.

And this quality of openness is not just a "Buddhist" phenomenon. It seems to characterize contemplatives in many traditions. Their actual experience in the divine or universal mystery seems to leave them very open to difference and, at the same time, they are acutely aware of that which is inviolable. This unusual mixture of flexibility and firmness seems to be a sign of genuine spiritual maturity, and it is the hallmark of a healthy contemplative. If that is not our experience, though—if we feel somewhat rigid or wishy-washy in our spirituality—we needn't fret about it. Awareness of our need for growth is like a compass. It helps to guide us into the contexts that we require in order to move forward in our lives and away from the contexts that inhibit our growth. It is cause for celebration rather than criticism.

# CHAPTER TWO

# When the Need for Love Meets the Great Unfixables

My mother groan'd! my father wept.
Into the dangerous world I leapt:
Helpless, naked, piping loud,
Like a fiend hid in a cloud.

Struggling in my father's hands,
Striving against my swaddling bands,
Bound and weary, I thought best
To sulk upon my mother's breast.
William Blake

We begin life struggling with the enormous gap between the way we imagine we need things to be and the way things are. It is here at birth that the pain of injustice is first felt; our first encounter with the conflict between the way things are and the way we feel they ought to be. The first and the most terrifying trauma of life is the loss of our comfortable home inside of our mothers' bodies, where needs were met automatically. It is the trauma of being thrust, without permission or warning, into a bizarre, cold world, where absolutely everything feels out of order and upsetting.

And this strange new inescapable thing called "the world" is now always here, always intruding, waking us up from the dream. And so the infant begins to cry.

Infancy is a scary and vulnerable time for humans: human beings have very large brains and very complex nervous systems and so it takes extra time and special, highly "pampered" conditions for these to develop. Developments like the ability to move around and care for one's bodily needs all take a back seat to the development of the brain. And this makes human beings unusually dependent on their mothers and fathers.

This is a very different story than what we see in less large-brained mammals, like horses, for example. When a baby horse is born, he or she is a little awkward at first, but is soon up and walking. And other, even simpler, animals are even more immediately competent. Many species of reptiles and amphibians abandon their eggs once they are laid. But human beings are a much more fragile and sensitive type of animal. We need a parental love that—for the most part—is unconditional or we simply can't survive.

The wonderful and amazing thing is that human infants often do seem to get the unconditional love that they need. More ordinary experiences of love include some element of transaction, in which I "love" you because of what I get from you, and if I stop getting what I want, my "love" for you begins to fade.

In premodern times, experiences like the kind of unconditional love a parent has for a child were viewed with a greater sense of mystery. They were understood as something divine, as the infused love of God, or, at least, as a gift of God. Many contemporary thinkers suggest, though, that what we often imagine to be "unconditional love" is in fact highly "conditioned" in one way or another—by our biology, our society, our desire to appear perfect, or a combination of such forces. Critical perspectives like these can help us discover that, at times, certain very unloving conditions may be at work behind that experience we quickly label "unconditional love"—behind it may be myriad evolutionary urgings, society's imposition of unattainable ideals on women, and even a kind of selflessness which is, at bottom, self-destructive or self-aggrandizing. Yet despite all this, we need to keep our hearts open to the possibility of encountering a spiritual mystery, a love that is truly not conditioned.

## Love and Grasping

The Buddha's teachings on this subject take a somewhat different approach. They simply observe that sometimes what we call "unconditional love" is evidently present, and at other times it is not. The Buddha taught that those who have developed their full potential as human beings "abide" in this sort of love. The word he used to describe the consciousness of those who abided in unconditional love was "godly" or "divine." The Pali term for this is *brahma vihara*, or "divine abiding." The word "divine" within Buddhist teachings is not understood as being something outside of the realm of the mind, some characteristic possessed, for instance, by gods but not humans. In fact, divine qualities are understood to be the core potentials of human consciousness. Although they are not always known experientially because the experience of them must be cultivated, they are still always present as potentials. "Divine" beings are thus those who have more fully cultivated awareness of these core potentials.

The divine abodes are four interrelated emotional qualities that together make up the Buddhist understanding of love that is not conditioned.

- Unconditioned goodwill (*metta*); goodwill is the desire for the other's flourishing as a human being.
- Unconditioned compassion (*karuna*); compassion is the desire for the resolution of the other's suffering.
- Unconditioned joy in the other's happiness (*muditha*).
- Unconditioned emotional security, or equal-mindedness, in the face of change (*upekkha*).

It should also be noted that unconditioned goodwill is different than desiring for others to have whatever they want and that unconditioned compassion is different than desiring to "make the suffering of others go away."

These are not ordinary, goal-oriented emotions; nor are they created, sustained, or eliminated based only on a limited set of specific conditions. There can, however, be obstacles to their perceptibility and manifestation within consciousness. There are three important aspects of the brahma viharas: Firstly, they are not conceptual ideals, which one strives to emulate—rather they are descriptions of dynamic processes that are actually present within the mind. Secondly, they influence our understandings, judgments, decisions, and actions in a seamless way. Their expression in action is thus fluid, not a mechanical step in which one "applies" what one "feels" and "thinks best." Thirdly, they are not developmental processes, which have an origin in historical, biological, psychological, or social causes and conditions. They are transcendental processes, which do not have an origin or an end. Awareness of the brahma viharas, however, is a developmental process, which has causes and conditions and may be obstructed, delayed, facilitated, and so on.

The kind of affection that is associated with our more ordinary or mundane level of consciousness is referred to in Buddhism as "grasping" rather than love, because its primary concern is with the achievement of the ego's goals or the gratification of its desires. The affection of grasping is not stable and dependable. If the grasping ego's goals are not met, its affection can quickly turn into hostility or indifference. Unlike mature love, its affection is highly conditioned—which is to say highly dependent on conditions.

The psychological contrast between the Buddhist views of grasping and love are similar to what Jewish theologian Martin Buber described as the contrast between the relational dimensions he called the "I-It" and the "I-Thou." In the "I-It" relation, the "I" relates to a person, or to the self, or to the environment, as a kind of object that only exists to benefit or frustrate the "I." It is a completely instrumental relationship. In contrast, in the "I-Thou" relation, the "I" relates to the other as a whole being like itself, which can only be understood through a reverent, non-exploitive dialogue between partners of equal value. There are also some similarities between the Buddhist view of love and grasping and the Christian view of divine love (called *caritas/agape* in Latin/Greek) and human love (called *phileo* and *eros*). What the Buddha's teachings add to Buber's perspective is that between the "I-It" and the "I-Thou" there is a radical transformation, a reorientation of identity, as the horizon of the mind is expanded. The "I" of the "I-It" encounter is thus not the *same* "I" that manifests in the "I-Thou" encounter. The different perception of the Other reflects a different level of consciousness, in which the Other is no longer an "It." Still, that Other, which has become a "Thou" through a transformation in the level of consciousness, may be a human being, a squirrel, a stone, or a mountain.

In later chapters, we will explore specific teachings on different levels of consciousness and how they relate to experiencing love and grasping.

## Basic Spiritual Needs

Each of the divine abodes points to one of four basic and inter-related spiritual needs. These four needs penetrate every aspect of our lives—the physical, emotional, social, vocational—and also point to something that is unconditioned or transcendent, beyond time and space. Like the needs for adequate physical nourishment and shelter, these four qualities point to qualities of mind that are not optional, but essential, for human flourishing:

- the need for genuine goodwill (an unconditional concern for our happiness), rather than a goodwill that disappears or is withdrawn by the other when certain conditions are not met.
- the need for genuine compassion (an unconditional concern for the relief of our suffering), rather than a compassion that disappears or is withdrawn by the other when certain conditions are not met.
- the need to see our happiness causing genuine joy in others, rather than causing greed, envy, resentment, or hatred.
- the need to be received as we actually experience ourselves to be, rather than as an other wishes us to be, and rather than as an object of their grasping, aversion, or indifference.

Together, these four describe the human need for a love that is, in a word, truly unconditioned.

## Life's Vicissitudes

There are of course times when some things are exactly the way that we wish them to be. But then, always, something happens.

Something changes. The beautiful sense of harmony and order that we were enjoying is disrupted, replaced by something unexpected. Often the first thing that we come to understand about life, in a deep, visceral way, is that it just keeps moving on and changing in ways that are beyond our control. It is constantly in flux.

The Buddha used the word *lokadharma* to describe this ever-changing quality of life. It is often translated into English as "the vicissitudes of life." It describes the continual starts and stops that we experience in life. We typically experience them at the level of gross physical sensations, emotions, and interactions, as shifts between pleasure and pain, gain and loss, praise and blame, popularity and rejection, and other such dualities. But we experience lokadharma also on the more subtle levels of existence, down to the continual molecular changes of the physical world, and beyond. The Buddha emphasizes that, at all levels of existence, the experiences that we like simply do not remain as long as we wish. And the experiences that we do not like do not leave as quickly as we wish. An integral aspect of the nature of existence seems to be that it simply does not obey our wishes. This is the way it is; there is no one to blame for this. And, even if we do find someone or something to blame for this, and then destroy, punish, educate, or somehow alter that alleged cause of our suffering, it will not change the fact that existence does not obey our wishes. Still the desire to find someone/something that is to blame for this fact, and someone/something that can fix it, runs very deep.

As infants, our parents try to protect us from disruption as much as possible, but some things are simply beyond even their control. And when things aren't as we want them to be, we cry. It is true that, in time, through the maturation process and with the help of our parents, we learn how to gain more control over many of life's vicissitudes. And we learn a broader array of strategies for coping, beyond simply crying. But the nature of life itself—its tendency to keep moving through vicissitudes—never changes. And so, no matter how much skill we develop at preventing unwanted changes, we continue to find that often in life things are still not as we wish they were, not as we feel they should be. Despite the fantasies of children, this gap does not just disappear somehow when we become adults.

For example, one moment we may be enjoying a relaxing moment of privacy, and, suddenly, a person who we are not particularly fond of pops by, or a telemarketer calls, or the pain in our knee starts acting up. So many of life's vicissitudes remain beyond our control. And actually, when it comes to the most profoundly difficult conditions in life—such as our physical decline, the loss of our loved ones, and our own impending death—we ultimately lack any real control at all. They are unpreventable and unfixable. The unique pain called dukkha arises out of this gap between our need for that which is limitless and the reality of life's vicissitudes. We are left with this unanswered longing, and experientially it feels like a painful wound.

Since our encounters with such difficult conditions cannot possibly be eliminated, we very wisely begin to wonder: "How can these encounters be best related to?" It is that question that rings at the heart of the Buddha's first noble truth, the truth of dukkha. Life inevitably frustrates us, and unless we find a beneficial way to relate to its frustrations, especially the unfixable ones, they create an invisible wound, a misery that prevents us from flourishing. The wound of dukkha can feel incurable. It is curable, which is the whole point of the Buddha's story, but that is getting too far ahead for the moment.

# CHAPTER THREE

# The Flight from Pain into Fantasy

The desire of the moth for the star,
Of the night for the morrow,
The devotion to something afar
From the sphere of our sorrow...
Percy Bysshe Shelley

Have you ever noticed that anyone who
drives slower than you is an idiot, and anyone
who drives faster than you is a maniac?
George Carlin

In this chapter, we'll explore the second truth of the Buddha's Dharma, which he called *tanha,* or "thirst." The Buddha taught that we inevitably react with tanha to the predicament of the first truth (dukkha), and that this reaction, in the long run, makes things worse instead of better. Tanha is also translated into English as "desire." And it is "desire," but a very complex kind of desire. For example, it is the kind of desire that allows one to spend years of one's life not wanting to say "goodbye" to someone who has already left one's life. Or refusing to acknowledge some unwanted experience that is already present in one's life. Tanha is the kind of desire that militates against the reality of the way things are by creating its own imaginary world and refusing to leave that fantasy, so as to not be wounded any further. And this is what makes it so complex.

## Impermanence, Vulnerability, and Pain

By carefully observing the vicissitudes of his life, and how he himself reacted to them, the Buddha noticed that there were certain polarities that seemed to be always with him, like a continuous thematic thread running through his experiences:

- There was a thirst for a permanent, unconditioned source capable of meeting basic spiritual needs. But despite this wish, he noticed that the reality he actually experienced was one of the impermanence and conditionality of all phenomena (*anicca*), including his own physical and mental being.

- There was a thirst for a stable self, which could have actual control over the vicissitudes of life, so that it could guarantee the meeting of his basic needs. But despite this wish, he noticed that, just like other phenomena, he himself had a highly vulnerable nature, which had little actual power over the critical vicissitudes of life that affected him. This is the reality of *anatta*.

- There was a thirst for a well-being (*sukha*) that could endure all of the actual experiences of life. But despite this wish, he noticed that what was actually always with him, even in his most pleasant experiences, was a subtle sense of trouble, or underlying pain (dukkha).

Encountering these polarities leads to a profound panic in the human psyche, first felt at birth, but which we ordinarily continue to feel, in one form or another, throughout our lives. It is what Melanie Klein has described as the fear of our own annihilation. It arises as we are confronted with this chaotic situation where our needs for permanence and security are met by a world that is constantly in flux. We face what may feel like an absurd mismatch between our needs and the reality of existence.

Very naturally, we bring all of our brainpower to bear on how to solve this core problem.

The ordinary way of responding to this existential panic, the Buddha observed, was to fall into a deep mental fantasy, an inner narrative, a waking dream, which helps one survive emotionally. The Buddha called this most basic survival narrative *samsara*.

Within the narrative of samsara, there is a common plot, which seeks to make our deepest wishes come true. There is a vision of a stable, satisfied self and there is a vision of a stable, satisfying object, which the stable self controls. Because of the way it speaks to our most basic emotional needs, this narrative generates an illusory sense of peace, a sense that our core conflict in life has been resolved. Our basic anxiety, the fear of our annihilation, seems briefly or intermittently to dissipate, and we feel safe. The spirit of samsara and its pervasive nature are beautifully captured in the poem quoted above by Shelley.

This fantasy of samsara soothes us. This is why, with our amazing brains, we create it. But, since it cannot change the actual nature of life, the peaceful spell that it casts on us continues to be broken, over and over again, by life's vicissitudes. Unpleasantness, loss, blame, rejection, and the like continually break through our enchantment and re-kindle our basic anxiety, which began at birth—the mismatch of the way we want to things to be and the way things are.

For the Buddha, the fantasy of samsara was among the most important things in life to come to terms with, because it clarified the critical missing piece in our struggles as human beings. Between the points of birth and death, there was only one central predicament that applied to every human experience. All other conflicts and problems were derivative of this core existential issue, because it was the heart of human suffering. In the first of the four truths, the Buddha had understood that our predicament began with how our need for an unconditioned reality was perpetually frustrated by the constantly changing nature of all phenomena. Now, in the second truth, he understood that, because life's seeming indifference to our needs is so terribly anxiety-provoking, we construct powerful stories in our minds to convince ourselves that it isn't so. These stories convince us of two things: (1) that at the core of our experience is a fundamental inadequacy; and (2) that impermanent objects (mistakenly seen as permanent) are both the cause of and the cure for that inadequacy. The samsaric stories we tell enslave us to an insatiable desire for objects, for something outside ourselves—to possess them, to destroy them, to avoid them. And that desire maintains and strengthens the dual illusion we have about a fundamental inadequacy and the great power of objects to either repair or destroy it.

The unfortunate irony then became clear: how could the solution to suffering—whatever it might be—be uncovered without facing, making peace with, exploring, and actually coming to understand the vicissitudes of life as it is and ourselves as we are? The very thing that we ordinarily do in life to secure greater peace of mind—i.e. constructing samsaric stories—is what ultimately prevents us from resolving the conflict beneath all conflicts. Our "solution" turns out to be the heart of the problem. Because of it, we never come to actually know, face to face, the true nature of what it is that we are running from, what it is that we are running toward, and who we actually are.

## The Evolution of Character

The Buddha taught that, within the swirl of life's vicissitudes, what the mind repeatedly inclines toward and acts upon, over time, becomes our character. Ordinarily, we tend to incline our minds toward what we imagine will best meet our basic needs, most broadly conceived. Thus, character is like a highly individualized prescription, written over a lifetime, for how we imagine our basic needs can best be met.

To determine what will meet those needs, we ordinarily rely upon our memories; especially memories of strategies that we feel came close to meeting our needs in the past, and memories of experiences that seriously failed to. Throughout life, we collect these special memories, and, out of them, we construct a mental story about who we are and what we need and how we hope to find fulfillment in the future. This inner story functions like the "automatic pilot" on an airplane. It guides us and shapes our reasoning from behind the scenes.

In another sense, character is essentially a highly practiced personal narrative in which we are the hero. Indeed, the narrative is so highly practiced, and practiced out of such great need, that it becomes our virtual self, our very understanding of who we are. So, for example, a person with a character that is very patient is one who has come to understand, again and again through life experiences, that the most effective way to meet his/her basic needs is by calming the mind, by waiting, rather than protesting or complaining. A person with a character that is very hostile is one who has come to understand, again and again through life experiences, that the most effective way to meet his/her basic needs is by demanding, threatening, and taking what is wanted. Character concentrates our attention on those aspects of life that we feel will bring us what we want, and away from those aspects of life that are less promising, or threatening.

No matter what form it takes—hostile or patient, shy or showy, moral or immoral—character accomplishes something very important for the person. Character gives the vicissitudes of life—especially our own internal ups and downs—the appearance of being somewhat under control: *our* control. Through character, we present a stable front to the world and shield ourselves from a great deal of turbulence. And this is a great achievement because, with this increased sense of control, we have found a way for our lives to feel less chaotic and fragile. In character, we have created a respite for ourselves, a temporary sanctuary from change, a place where we have determined that, for the most part, things will always be the same, no matter what.

And this naturally has a profoundly soothing effect on our need for an unchanging reality.

But even this changes.


## The Myth of the Yogis

The Buddha used a powerful myth to shed light on the process of how we move from the disturbing awareness of our basic anxiety to a more comfortable experience of character. It describes the actual yogic practices of ancient India, but it is mythic in the sense of how he used it to convey a meaning much broader and deeper than the actual historical details.

India in the sixth century BCE was full of yogis, spiritual practitioners engaging in different kinds of yoga. *Yoga*, in Sanskrit, has a much broader meaning than the contemporary use of the word. *Yoga* means "yoke" or "union," and it refers to the ultimate spiritual quest of union with the divine, where ultimate well-being was found. In this sense everyone has a yoga; our yoga is our deepest understanding of what well-being is and how it can be realized in life. Everyone is engaged in this quest in his or her own way. Of course, some yogas are better than others. For example, the person who finds well-being through intoxicating the body until it can only feel pleasure and the person who finds well-being through being a good neighbor are both pursuing a yoga, but one leads to greater fragmentation in the mind, rather than to greater unity and order. In the Buddha's time, yoga was classified very broadly into two categories—pain yoga and pleasure yoga.

Pain yoga was about techniques for getting rid of or moving away from those aspects of life that separated one from the divine. The yogic object, or Other—the thing upon which the yogi focused—was a negative thing that the yogi sought to eliminate. For example, the yogic object might be the experience of greed, and the related yogic practices might involve severe fasting in an attempt to eliminate greed. This was called "pain yoga" because it envisioned happiness as involving a relationship between the yogi and an object thought to cause ultimate pain.

*Ego-identity experience in pain yoga*

Whenever the yogi could destroy, or escape from, this pain-causing object, there was an emotional release, a sense of peace, and at times even an ecstasy or grandiosity. Otherwise he lived in fear and resentment of these objects, humiliated by his failure to eliminate them. His sense of well-being is sustained by his aversion.

Pleasure yoga, the other category of yoga, was about moving closer to and possessing those aspects of life that united one with the divine. The yogic object was a positive thing, which the yogi sought to constantly stay in the presence of. For example, the yogic object might be the imagined smiling face of his guru, or a virtue, such as patience. This was called "pleasure yoga" because it envisioned ultimate well-being as involving a relationship between the yogi and an object thought to cause ultimate pleasure. Whenever the yogi possessed, or was possessed by, such an object, there was an emotional release. Otherwise, he lived in grief and longing for these objects, humiliated by his failure to continuously possess them. His sense of well-being is sustained by his clinging.

*Ego-identity experience
in pleasure yoga*

Both types of yoga involved a relationship between the yogi and the yogic object. They only differed in the nature of the object and the nature of the relationship. If the nature of the object was pleasant, the nature of the relationship between the yogi and the yogic object was one of clinging. If the nature of the object was unpleasant, then the nature of the relationship between the yogi and the yogic object was one of aversion.

This was a very graphic thing in ancient India. There were living metaphors, archetypes, on the streets of what the Buddha was portraying. In those days, one could readily see groups of yogis submitting themselves to painful ascetic regimes, and others who looked like they were lost in clouds of bliss as they gazed into the eyes of their master.

The myth conveys two basic things that are important to notice and understand in relation to the human predicament:

1. These yogas involve a relationship between the yogi and a yogic object.
2. These relationships exist primarily in the mind of the yogi.

The teachings of the Buddha suggest that the dramas of these preoccupied yogis are precisely the dramas that take place within the privacy of our minds the majority of the time. They describe the dynamic process of how character develops and is sustained as an attempted solution to the basic anxiety of our human predicament.

The psychological process unfolds something like this: An image arises in my mind. It is an image of myself, an imaginary replica of me. It is not really who I am; it is just an image that exists in thought. It represents me, like a painting of the ocean represents the ocean, but is not really the ocean. It looks and feels completely like me, though, because it has been constructed out of my memories of past experiences.

This image of myself that arises in the mind never arises in isolation. It always arises in relation to some mental object. In the case of pleasure yoga, the image of myself arises, focusing on, captivated by, and drawn toward some pleasant object. The object might be a person, or a place, or a situation, or an idea, or a dream, or some material thing, or some complex combination of things. And the sense is that if this image of me, this virtual "self," can stay close to or somehow possess this object, whatever it is, then this "self" will be complete and at peace. Also, there is the corresponding sense that, without this object, this "self" will be incomplete, unhappy, or even in great distress.

So, in this scene within the mind, there is this ego-image, an image of myself as incomplete, not happy, not at peace. But also present in this mental scene is this image of a very powerful, pleasant object, which, in fantasy, can fulfill dreams, heal wounds, and provide happiness. The image of the empty subject and the image of the completing object arise together in the mind. Both are creations of thought. They exist only in the mind, as stories, about a "me" that is in need and an object that has the power to fulfill that need.

Because of the intensity of our needs, these internal creations of thought very naturally come to be misunderstood as real. The yogic object, which currently exists only in the mind, is mentally projected onto some external reality: for instance, the approving smile of a loved one. An actual smile on the face of the loved one then becomes identical with the yogic object in the mind. And the internal image of the pleasure yogi, the one-who-will-be-completely-fulfilled-by-the-object, is identified with who I myself actually am, with my body and mind, with my self. Psychologically, I then "become" the archetypal pleasure yogi. Through identification, the inert ego-image becomes a dynamic ego-state.

It becomes "me." And suddenly I find myself psychologically engrossed in a real-life drama about getting my loved one to always provide me with an approving smile. And so before this real, external physical person, my loved one, ever walked into the room, a drama was going on in my mind between the pleasure yogi and the object that it is sure will bring it ultimate fulfillment. The actual loved one was just inadvertently pulled into this ongoing mental drama. And in this way, pleasure yoga is enacted in my life. It starts in the mind, as an unrecognized fantasy, and then moves outward.

The flipside of this process is the way of pain yoga. Here, an image of myself arises in the mind—an imaginary replica of me, engaged in an imaginary scene. In this scene, the "self" is threatened by some object—a person, a situation, an emotion, a thought, or perhaps something material. The sense of drama is that if this "self" can get far enough away from, or somehow destroy, this object then there will be peace, and that as long as this object is near, this "self" will continue to be depleted, troubled, and unwell. The image of the empty subject and the image of the depleting object arise together in the mind. Both are creations of thought. They exist only in the mind, as stories, about a "me" that is in need, and an object that has the power to thwart that need. When this self-image in the mind is identified with, there is an enactment of the myth described by the Buddha in which the pain yogi is struggling internally with its unpleasant object. Then, inevitably, the unpleasant object in the mind is projected onto some external reality, such as the car that cuts the yogi off on the highway. The real-life drama that then ensues on the highway, which can sometimes result in actual violence, is an enactment of the archetypal pattern of pain yoga. The archetypal myth starts in the mind, as an unrecognized fantasy with which the person identifies, and then moves outward. And, although it sounds unusual, what the person is actually seeking through this entire process is happiness.

There also exists a third pattern or archetype of illusion, in addition to the archetypes governed by grasping or aversion. This yoga is governed by ignorance, which along with grasping and aversion, is one of the "three poisons" that cause suffering and obscure truth.

Imagine a third yogi, who is chronically apathetic and bored. The yogic object that arises in the mind in relation to this ego-image is an inert object. This object is not useful to the ego; it does her no good to possess it; it does her no good to destroy it. It just does her no good, period. And so, the apathetic yogi's pre-occupation is with seeking anything else but this distracting, useless object.

In many school contexts, the boy or girl who doesn't wear designer clothes, doesn't have a designer personality, isn't tough

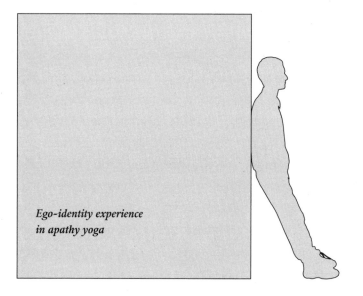

*Ego-identity experience*
*in apathy yoga*

enough to inspire fear, and isn't unusual enough to inspire bullying just becomes "invisible." We could describe this as an example of the yoga of apathy. The object—in this case a person—is simply not seen because it is of no value to the ego. We can probably think of many other examples of people, even ourselves, engaging in apathy yoga.

Here, like before, the image of the empty subject and the image of the inert object arise together in the mind. Both are creations of thought. They exist only in the mind, as stories about a "me" that is in need and an object that, in this case, has the power to distract me from those objects that I imagine can either fulfill or thwart my need.

In the Buddha's psychology of human suffering, these archetypal patterns described in the myth of the yogis are continually spinning within the mind. As a result, conscious awareness then virtually becomes a series of reactions to certain images of the self and certain desirable and undesirable objects. And it is through the spinning of these narratives that the unique shape of our character comes into existence. Character, in the Buddhist understanding, is thus a kind of mechanical or computational structure.

In the language of machines, we could say that the myth of the yogis describes the basic algorithm that runs the engine of character. What happens to this algorithm in the process of spiritual development is one of the most interesting themes in the Buddhist psychology of transformation. As we will see later, we should not be too quick to purge it from the mind.

For our purposes now, it is important to note that this algorithm is not "alive," it is not the "real" us, it is just a very complex, highly practiced pattern of habitual reactions. It is, however, a kind of virtual self, because it is "who" we most often understand and experience ourselves to be.

The three forms of yoga we've looked at above can serve to describe the nature of tanha, the nature of the insatiable thirst, or desire, which is the root cause of suffering. The myth teaches us that tanha is the dualistic desire of an empty subject to possess completing objects (Others), to escape or destroy depleting objects (Others), and to ignore inert objects (Others). This duality of subject and object, and the desire it generates, however, is not real; it only exists within the narrative world of samsara.

## Ego and Samsara

Whenever these images of oneself that arise in the mind, constructed out of memories and wishes, are unconsciously taken to be real, they are what the Buddhist tradition calls "ego." In other words, the ego is the conviction that character is a real self, a living being who is "in charge" of one's life, not simply a collection of mechanical habits. Egoic consciousness refers to consciousness that is being regulated by the illusion that character is the living, breathing essence of who we are. To prevent confusion, it is important to note that this is quite a different understanding of the word "ego" than is found in popular culture or within psychoanalysis, where it may refer to a more benign and helpful aspect of personality.

The mental objects, arising with the ego, refer to subjective ideals of one form or another. They are the objects that are longed for (positive ideals) because, it is hoped, they will make the ego complete, and the objects that are hated (negative ideals) because, it is feared, they will make the ego more impoverished and fragmented.

So in the myth of the yogis we see a glimpse inside of ordinary, or egoic, consciousness. Ordinary consciousness is encased in character and regulated by it. Ordinary consciousness only sees what character believes is important to be seen. If patience is important, it sees opportunities for patience. If conquest and domination are important, it sees opportunities for conquest and domination. Both traditional morality and traditional immorality have their foundation in character, in the imaginary mental dramas of the ego and its objects.

The Buddha's radical suggestion is that the myth of the yogis is the very foundation of ordinary personal life, family life, business, societal structures, governments, religions, and so on; this myth reveals the symbolic structure of the world order that human beings have created. All human societies, institutions, families, and individuals—unless they wake up from their spiritual slumber—mindlessly follow the narrative patterns of pain yoga, pleasure yoga, and apathy yoga. And within these patterns, as we will see, human agency is systematically distorted, since there is no awareness of the more subtle, transcendental aspects of reality beyond the metaphysical beliefs of the ego.

We spoke above about samsara, the inner fantasy or narrative that we create to help us cope with the fact that the world is constantly changing, in spite of our need for an unchanging reality. The myth of the yogis is simply another tool that the Buddha used for explaining the breadth and depth of samsara. The myth helps us understand samsara as the "master plot" for the many stories that get composed in our minds to foster the illusion that the objects we are pursuing are real, permanent, and will completely and forever satisfy our needs.

And so, in all of this, the Buddha is further exposing the nature of the human predicament. He is suggesting, "Look for this plot, described in the myth of the yogis. Anywhere you find it, you will find suffering." And, unfortunately, we find it built into the very structure of our character, our family, our society, our religion... We find it everywhere, because it is the foundation of ordinary consciousness. The good news about this, however, is that our fundamental problem is not at all unique. It is the predicament of every human being.

We have to be cautious here, though, to not conclude that this plot of samsara is something unnatural, evil, or the "enemy" of humankind, because without this plot we never would have survived the traumatic realizations we inevitably experience as human beings. Samsara, or egoic consciousness, literally helps us stay alive and well. It also gives rise to much of what we understand as civilization. It is not simply a one-dimensional force that fosters human degradation. Samsara itself can mature, become more attuned and responsive to the subtlety of human needs. It can foster a more skillful way of life that actually promotes our flourishing—at least up to a certain point.

Earlier, in describing the myth of the yogis, the point was made that some yogic objects are better than others—the person whose quest for happiness focuses on getting intoxicated and the person whose quest focuses on being a good neighbor are both pursuing a yoga—but that while one leads to greater degradation, the other leads to greater unity and coherence. Both persons portrayed were deeply entrenched in the root narrative of samsara, enacting its patterns, and yet one of them was moving in the direction of degradation, while the other was moving toward greater flourishing as a human being. In Buddhist terminology, one was accruing negative karma, while the other was accruing positive karma. Accruing karma involves cultivating habits of character that are either not helpful (negative karma) or helpful (positive karma) with respect to the ultimate goal of transcending the limited, patterned, egoic consciousness called samsara. It seems contradictory, but without our "membership" in samsara we would not be able to develop the level of personal skill that puts us in a position to transcend samsara. Without misunderstanding our character as being a true self, capable of controlling its destiny by pursuing objectives that are truly beneficial and declining to pursue objectives that are truly harmful, we never evolve to the point of realizing that, though once useful, this myth is actually a misunderstanding of the way things actually are, which is preventing our further development and flourishing.

Tanha, the second truth of the Buddha's Dharma, can lead us toward the realization that egoic consciousness, at certain points in our evolution, is what prevents us from being fully alive. It is the root cause of much of our civilization, and thus helpful. But it is also the root cause of our greed, hatred, indifference, and injustice, and thus not helpful.

We hear in the second truth that the vicissitudes of our lives—the wet diapers, the telemarketer calling at dinner time, the diagnosis of a serious illness, and so on—are not the root problem. Our need for an unconditioned reality is also not the root problem. The root problem, which we do need to be liberated from, whenever we are ready, is our identification with the plot of samsara. Our root predicament is that this plot is defining who we are and telling the story of our lives. And because of this process, we become empty subjects, filled with illusory desires that keep us chasing after the objects we hope will complete us, fleeing from the objects we fear will destroy us, and simply not valuing or paying attention to anything else.

It is important to be clear that the root problem identified in the second truth is not the development of character itself. We need character, and, in fact, much of the Dharma path is focused on its refining, on training ourselves in virtue. The root problem is the illusion that surrounds character, where we see it as essentially "me." It helps to keep in mind the distinction made earlier between character and ego. Character is only a mechanical, habitual process. Ego is the false sense of self that comes to dominate consciousness when character is misunderstood as being the autonomous, living center of our being, the core of who we are.

It is also important to be clear that until we are moving beyond even the aspiration of accruing positive karma, we do not become fully free from samsara. Positive karma is, in a sense, "the bright side" of samsara—but it is still samsara. It is still egoic consciousness. But it is the very best—the maximum flourishing— that egoic consciousness can offer human beings in their process of evolution. As we will see in chapter 4, one of the most intriguing aspects of the fourth truth—the path—is that, on our way toward greater ego transcendence, we end up engaging significantly in the myth of karma, and thus getting the best that the ego has to offer. As we follow the path, we are always engaged in one of two processes. Either we are accruing good karma by constructing a better—more flexible, sensitive, and ethically oriented— character, which we still imagine to be our essential self, or we are transcending that illusion about who we are. Either way, it is a "win/win" proposition, both for the individual practitioner, and the world that surrounds him or her.

The second truth, tanha, in a nutshell teaches that the root cause of suffering, the root of the human predicament, is this phenomenon of ego. And now we can see why it is such a "predicament"— because this root cause is woven into the very structure of ordinary consciousness. And so there is no exit, no real solution to it, without an alternative level of consciousness.

In this way, through realizing this second truth, the Buddha's understanding of his predicament as a human being was deepened. He had identified its root cause. And having understood that the cause was not simple, but interwoven into the very structure of ordinary consciousness, he now faced the question of whether or not there could possibly be a cure. Could consciousness actually be liberated from the plot of samsara? Was there any actual alternative to egoic consciousness?

# CHAPTER FOUR

# Home Is Where We Flourish

In the experience of dukkha (chapter 2), we have a very tight grip on who we think we are, and we perceive that our identity is threatened by the vicissitudes of life. In the understanding of tanha (chapter 3), that identity, which we fear losing, is seen to be illusory. The "one" whose annihilation is threatened by the vicissitudes of life is essentially a narrative character, which only exists in thought. Still, nothing could feel more real than this narrative character. When we identify ourselves as it, that character comes to life as the dynamic ego. It installs itself as the official owner and operator of the mind, and goes about getting control of all of the objects it sees as capable of either enhancing or threatening its rule.

In the realization of nirodha, which is the focus of this fourth chapter, we realize experientially that it is not possible to fully flourish as a human being when our awareness of who we are is confined to this inner narrative of the ego and its objects. *Nirodha* literally means "cessation" (specifically cessation of tanha) but it is far more nuanced than that single word implies. As we come to see nirodha, the illusions of tanha gradually lose their attractiveness, awareness disengages from its identification with the ego; with full realization of this nirodha we become able to experience the blissful purity of the mind itself. We understand then that our former perception of the gap between our need for an unconditioned reality and the vicissitudes of life was itself conditioned by an illusion about who we are. The painful experience of the gap was created by our identification with the plot of samsara. Without that illusory identification, we are no longer the empty subject; the problematic gap, and the suffering it produces, cease to exist.

The truth of nirodha opens up the mystery of our identity, the awareness of which has been lost in the many fear-based definitions of ourselves and our world. The moment that anyone—including ourselves—has our identity "all figured out," we can be certain that we are deep in illusion. From the Buddha's point of view, the truth of who we are is beyond the scope of ordinary knowledge. In his spiritual awakening, rather than discovering a more precisely defined self, he became more aware of the fact that his identity was an ineffable, uncategorizable mystery.

Something happens when we understand at an experiential level what the ego is, and we recognize that we are not the ego. Awakening to the truth of nirodha is initiated by understanding who we are not, but have perhaps have always thought that we were. It is an awakening of identity, but not identity in a definitive, boundaried, narrative, historical, or conceptual sense. It is an awareness of identity on a level that transcends individual character. It is a much lighter, and yet a much more profound, awareness of who we are.

Nirodha is an encounter with the pure mind itself, beneath the dualistic illusion of tanha, outside of the narrative world of samsara. When we are aware of nirodha, our sense of who we are is transformed in a way that is difficult to put into words. It is not that who we have always taken ourselves to be is somehow "gone." We still have an awareness of being a unique person, who was born of certain parents, grew up in a certain neighborhood, has certain strengths and problems and dreams, and so on. But we also have an awareness that the very nature of our life is transcendent, is other than these details. Our horizon has expanded, and our historical character is no longer its center. We no longer see only through the eyes of that character that had been our sole identity. Nirodha is the place in the mind where the ineffable mystery of our identity is experienced. And though the question "if I am not the ego, then who am I?" is not "answered" in any concrete way, there is an understanding within which that question ceases to apply. And to our surprise, when egoic consciousness ceases we discover we are not at all out of control, unintelligent, or in danger of losing our well-being without the ego's regulating consciousness. In fact, we experience a sense of coherence, wisdom, and joy that is far deeper than any we have known in even our best states of egoic consciousness.

Our character remains but is no longer the "automatic pilot" of consciousness, because it is no longer unwittingly experienced as the deep mysterious essence of who we really are.

## Where Is Home?

In ordinary, egoic consciousness, our "home" is a certain kind of mental narrative in which we are the hero, pursuing objects that promise to make us whole and fleeing from or destroying objects that threaten our fragmentation and degradation.

The objects in these personal narratives can be sophisticated and civilized; they can be seeking "a good education," "personal enlightenment," or "world peace," and avoiding "self-destructive habits." Conversely, the objects in the narrative can be thoroughly barbaric; they can be seeking to exterminate our political "enemies," and avoiding any potential awareness of our vulnerability.

These are extreme examples, but the point is that some narrative homes are clearly more hospitable, peaceful, and better organized than others. The quality of that home in the mind depends largely on the quality of the objects, and the related ego-images, that make it up. But often, tragically, no matter how much suffering it causes, "home is home." We become accustomed to a certain inner narrative, and despite its drawbacks, we often feel more comfortable within it than we do in an objectively more hospitable one. Our inner narratives have been designed to soothe our basic needs, and to do so in ways that create the least anxiety for us. Reconstructing our personal narratives to make them more hospitable places in which to live is a challenging but necessary and helpful practice, one that is creatively integrated into the fourth truth of the path.

But here in the third truth of his Dharma, the Buddha went beyond that reconstructive approach to clearly establish nirodha as that place within the mind that is not narrative or conceptual in nature and yet is our truest home. It is a home that cannot die or be destroyed, because it was never constructed or created in the first place. It was already there before we were born. It will always be there, even after we die. It is spacious. It is blissful. It is secure. It does not fluctuate in response to the vicissitudes of life, because it is located outside of time and history and the realm of conditioned reality. Nirodha describes what remains in consciousness, what we become aware of as being actually present when the illusions of samsara—the fantasies of the ego and its objects—break up and cease to cloud the mind. Nirodha is that breakthrough into awareness of the true nature of the mind itself.

Grounded in this awareness of the true nature of the mind itself, the human predicament ceases to exist. The vicissitudes of life—pain and pleasure, gain and loss, popularity and rejection, praise and blame, and all such dualities—continue, as ever, to fluctuate. But they no longer pose a threat to the mind that is grounded in awareness of its true nature.

Accordingly, nirodha is also traditionally known as "the Deathless" or "the Unconditioned."

## Expanding the Horizon of Ancient India

For years the Buddha had explored and practiced in depth the various dharmas of his day. And he had learned several important things from various teachers, but none completely led him to freedom. Until now, he had not encountered a different level of consciousness, which transformed his actual experience of the human predicament. And now he understood why. He began to reflect on the problems in the religious practices of his day.

The various dharmas that he had learned, rather than being grounded in the actual experience of nirodha, focused on seeking a particular image of the divine (Brahma), an image that had been constructed, an image that—he now understood—was not different in its nature from the images of the ego and its objects. Those images were always a creation of thought. Moreover, the Buddha came to see that he himself—Siddhartha the spiritual seeker, who had given up everything, who had labored diligently at the feet of India's wisest masters, who had practiced many virtues and perfected many skills, the one he had always taken himself to be—was also a creation of thought. It was a character that had been constructed. In the light of nirodha, he could see this character clearly as it was, see its true nature. It was not a mysterious inner self that, through its noble efforts, had achieved unification with the divine. It was helpful, useful, beautiful, wonderful, but it was still an inanimate, fabricated, conceptual thing. And so not only was ultimate reality not what he had long imagined it to be, neither was he. What was he then? It was difficult for him to put into words. He was "awake." He was this awareness of nirodha, in which all of these realizations were unfolding. What was truly noble, he now saw, was this truth of nirodha and of dukkha and tanha that had finally opened up his mind.

When he realized that the dharmas of his day had their roots in samsara, specifically in the dominating egos of the ruling class, it was obvious why religion had become stuck. It could not get beyond the plane of ego consciousness. It was in fact perpetuating the very world order that spiritual life hoped to transcend and liberate humanity from. Out of this realization, he began the renewal movement in which, over the next forty years, he would teach the Dharma of the four truths that he had discovered.

## The Eclipse of Nirodha and the Dawn of Intelligence

True intelligence, as the Buddha understood it, is not related to intellectual cleverness, but to a cultivated sensitivity, which allows us to actually perceive the presence of dukkha, tanha, and nirodha in our everyday life experiences. Similarly, true ignorance has nothing to do with a lack of formal education. It is the result of a cultivated insensitivity to these basic truths, which is brought about by blindly following the inner plots driven by grasping, aversion, and ignorance.

Taken together, the three basic truths teach that all human misery has its roots in a consciousness that is clouded by this basic ignorance. We begin moving out of this ignorance and become more intelligent as we awaken to various realities in our everyday life experiences:

- the reality of our great vulnerability to life's vicissitudes: our finitude.
- the reality of our longing for an unchanging reality.
- the reality of our suffering that is related to (though not "caused" by) this clash between our vulnerability to impermanence and our longing for permanence.
- the reality of our fantasy's inability to bridge this gap, fulfill this longing, and solve this predicament.
- the reality that our historical character is actually a collection of habits, a mechanical, conditioned, reactive thing, that we have misunderstood as being who we are, as being the living "I," the "one" who, for example, is now sitting here and reflecting on these words.

As we more and more begin to notice this "I," it becomes clear that it is, in fact, not conscious, not the living master of our destiny, but a mechanical habit pattern. And with that realization, something very subtle and amazing can spontaneously occur: I can become experientially aware of the fact that I am observing this "I," this lifeless mechanism, and so I cannot possibly be this "I." I suddenly experience that the awareness that is observing this inanimate "I" is not the "I," is not mechanical, not reactive. And then, I begin to notice, perhaps for the first time in my life, the living intelligent nonreactive awareness that I actually am. A profound separation and differentiation then takes place in the mind. And I discover that my need for an unchanging reality no longer exists. My need for unconditioned goodwill, compassion, receptive joy, and stable security no longer exists. It is not that these needs have been "met" or "fulfilled." It is not that the needfulness is still there somewhere in my nature, but is momentarily appeased (like physical thirst). It is that it no longer exists, because that mental thirst belongs to the illusory realm of egoic consciousness. But personal agency remains, and awareness of it has now deepened; awareness has transcended that illusory level of the mind—egoic consciousness—that gives rise to those needs. We become aware that the "divine abodes" are present and active in consciousness. We experience a very subtle, gentle inner presence, which is watching everything that is, watching in a wise and compassionate way, and caring for all it watches as integral parts of the Whole of Life. Nirodha cannot be manufactured. It is, in fact, already present. The only effort involved is the effort of becoming sensitive enough to perceive it. Our sensitivity is dulled by unconsciously following the scripts of samsara, but as we begin training in consciously paying attention to our bodily and mental experiences, reflecting on them in light of dukkha, tanha, and nirodha, noticing that they are actually not under the ownership and control of a mysterious inner "I," our sensitivity to reality begins to grow. And increasingly we notice that we are experiencing this gentle presence of nirodha in the present moment.

But then, seemingly out of nowhere, a thought comes to mind about what might happen on the next episode of *Desperate Housewives*; or we wonder exactly how many grams of fat there really are in a Big Mac; or a worried thought arises about some aspect of our child's future education; or the neighbor's teenage son starts playing his drums in a way that seems obviously designed to stress us out. And suddenly, poof! we are back playing the familiar game of samsara again, looping around the endless circle of chasing and fleeing from objects, fueled by our most disintegrating anxieties. Our wonderful mystical experience seems miles and miles away, and we can't begin to imagine how we're ever going to get it back. Was nirodha only a dream? All we feel now is that the ego is back on its throne, and it's bored, or it's longing for something, or it's enraged about something, and it's manufacturing thoughts and emotions and full blown dramas faster than ever.

## The Path from Nirodha to Nirvana

Once we have encountered it, why does nirodha become eclipsed again by illusion? Why can't there be a permanent, once-and-for-all awakening to the pure and blissful nature of the mind? Why do we get catapulted back into the comparatively shallow and anxious identity of the ego? It feels painfully paradoxical to finally encounter an unchanging reality, our true home, and then just as we are getting ready to move in, to have it disappear into thin air.

The problem is that although we can clearly come to have tremendous insights and profound mystical experiences we still have a character that has been working night and day, for some number of years, according to the patterns of samsara. It knows—or it thinks it knows—exactly what we need, and when and how we need it. It knows what we should be afraid of, when we should start worrying about things, what we should be trying to get a hold of, and what we should struggle to get rid of. And it runs on automatic pilot, even in our dreams. So we can count on it to do its job—to flood our consciousness with reminders of everything that it thinks is important, instead of what is actually happening in the present moment.

Not only do we still have a character, we are still very accustomed to taking our character's activities very seriously and very personally. It plays a rerun in our minds of one of our favorite memories of chocolate, and we suddenly feel taken over by the conviction that we really deserve a hot fudge sundae. It flashes an image of our child with a frown on her face, and we start anxiously spinning a story in our minds about how we will never have enough money to put her through college. And so on. The automatic thoughts and emotions generated by character are identified with and then, as if by magic, the ego comes back to life as the center of consciousness, and our horizon constricts, anxiously narrow again.

We may have had a powerful transcendental experience simply in paying attention to our bodily experience in light of the Buddha's teachings. We do not want to minimize the significance of that, but we are going to need training to learn how to navigate in this strange new situation, where we can find ourselves moving in and out of different levels of consciousness. Not academic training, but the practical, experiential training of taking up a spiritual path. A spiritual path involves not just the practice of certain disciplines, like formal meditation; it is a comprehensive, integrated way of living that actively fosters the evolution of consciousness.

The fourth truth in the Buddha's Dharma—the taking up a spiritual path—is related to, but also quite different than, the transcendental encounter of the third truth: nirodha. A traditional analogy of the difference between the two compares the wonderful experience of falling in love with the actual realities of an ongoing intimate relationship that is conscious, healthy, caring, and beneficial.

When we fall in love, we frequently have the sense that there is already a wonderful, healthy, caring relationship present. We feel we couldn't possibly be flourishing more than we already are, and we see absolutely no obstacles to perfect, everlasting intimacy. But what we cannot see at that moment is that the actual encounter with the real human being involved may have only been for a millisecond, and that the bulk of our powerful reaction is rooted in our own personal fantasies about that millisecond encounter. The actual meeting with the real human being was like springing off of a diving board; it just facilitated our plunging into this wonderful pool of fantasy about having found our beloved. And so it's not surprising that new lovers often do seem like they've gone off the deep end!

Samsara gives perhaps its best performance in the experience of falling in love. The ego has found its ideal object—the exact one, the only one, it needs to be complete and fulfilled and happy forever and ever. In that moment, no one could convince us how much challenging work would be involved in having an actual relationship with this person. We can't imagine how anything related to such a divine creature could be like "work." But even if it did involve work, we would do absolutely anything for the beloved, because we are enthralled, enchanted, caught in a spell that we are certain will never be broken.

Compare that scenario with an actual love relationship that has been consciously cultivated over time, through pleasant and unpleasant experiences. There is mutuality, equality, and a sharing of the load. There is actual understanding of the other, as a being separate from my wishes and fantasies. There are well-cultivated, healthy patterns of communication. There is awareness of the other's deeper needs, fears, and hopes. There is actual joy when the other is happy. There is actual pain when the other suffers. There are rituals that celebrate togetherness and commitment. There is a primary desire for the other's well-being, rather than a primary desire for the other to meet my needs and wishes. There is respect and support for individuality and self-care. And so on.

It is obvious to us that a relationship of this quality is not something that one simply "falls into" unconsciously. It is something which is skillfully cultivated and which evolves over time. This contrast parallels the difference between the mystical experiences of nirodha, which may only be momentary, and experiencing the more stable and integrated reality of a spiritual way of life. It is only through the more disciplined experience of the fourth truth, the path, that we come to increasingly embody the wisdom of the first three truths.

When we are on the path and nirodha is in eclipse, we learn to deepen our sensitivity to what is happening in the present moment. The path guides us through an integrated system of training, which develops and strengthens our ability to do that. The purpose of the path is to keep the journey (from dukkha, through tanha, to nirodha) perpetually in motion. It helps us to recollect in the midst of actual life experiences what we have come to understand about the journey in these first four chapters. It stimulates our faith in the reality of nirodha, which is still present behind the clouds of illusion, and guides us through the process of penetrating those illusions, experiencing the pure nature of the mind, and grounding our awareness there.

When awareness no longer leaves its true home in the pure and blissful nature of the mind, it becomes wedded to nirodha, and then dukkha and tanha no longer reoccur. When such a union is established, the Buddha described it with the word "nirvana," which has the identical meaning as nirodha, except that it conveys a sense of finality. Thus, it is traditionally only used to describe the consciousness of a person whose experience no longer slides back into the illusions of samsara. For this reason, the path in the fourth truth is described as the path to nirvana.

# CHAPTER FIVE

# Self-Possession and Mature Spirituality

*Where the Middle Way Arises*

Recall from chapter 3 how the root problem identified in the second truth is not the development of character itself. We need character, and, in fact, an entire dimension of the upcoming fourth truth (the path) is focused on its training. Character itself, when it helps us to flourish, can be like a helpful companion in life. The root problem is an illusion that surrounds character. Again, it helps to keep in mind the distinction between character and ego: that character is a mechanical, habitual process and ego is the false sense of self. But we will not always keep this in mind. We will not always be experiencing the ego transcendence of nirodha. We will at times become the ego, and consciousness will be constricted to the horizon of our character. This is also part of the way things are. What we find, however, is that necessary spiritual growth takes place even within egoic consciousness, at the karmic level of character development.

We do not see the resolution of this apparent tension between the goal of transcendence and the goal of building a better character until we reach the fourth truth: the path. In the actual practice of the path, it becomes clear that the myth of karma is, in a sense, the bright side of samsara. It is still samsara. It is still egoic consciousness. But it is the very best—the maximum flourishing—that egoic consciousness can offer human beings in their process of evolution. One of the most intriguing aspects of the fourth truth is that, on our way toward greater ego transcendence, we end up engaging significantly in the myth of karma and thus getting the best that the ego has to offer. As we follow the path, there is no wasted motion. We are always engaged in one of two processes: either we are accruing positive karma by constructing a better—more flexible, sensitive, and ethically oriented —character, which we still imagine to be our essential self; or we are transcending that illusion about who we are, into the wise and virtuous bliss of nirodha. Either way, it is a "win/win" proposition for the individual practitioner and for the world that surrounds and includes him or her. Gradually this either/or quality evolves into a more complex mosaic, as our efforts to accrue positive karma for ourselves and those we care about become increasingly infused with insight about our true nature. Eventually even character is enlisted in fostering transcendence.

As we engage in reflecting on the first three truths, we recognize dukkha and tanha at an experiential level in our personal suffering, and therein discover nirodha as our liberation from that suffering. Actually experiencing such moments of liberation in our lives gives us realistic hope. And this hope, rather than encouraging a turning away from awareness of our finitude toward some future utopia, gives us the interest and the courage to remain in the present moments of our lives, and to reflect even more deeply on the truths of dukkha and tanha. Nirodha transcends the purely temporal realm of existence. It has no physical properties. Much of our lives, however, belong to this purely temporal realm. So how, then, can a transcendental reality like nirodha be knowable to us? Unless the Buddha could answer this very practical question, there could be no fourth noble truth, no integral practice, only philosophical insights. To appreciate the integrity between the philosophy (the first three truths) and its practice (the fourth truth), we will take a closer look in this section at the Buddha's basic anthropology—the understanding of human nature and experience in general implied by the Buddha's teachings.

In my view, it is at the points where the transcendental reality of nirodha and the temporal structure of human experience meet that the middle way—the spiritual path, the fourth of the Four Noble Truths—arises. The timeless dynamic of the path is nirodha, but its temporal form is the mature form of human experience in general. The spelling out of the practical details involved in this developmental process is one of the unique contributions made by the Buddha's teachings.

One of the most important meanings of the Pali word *sati* (usually translated as "attention" or "mindfulness") is "self-possession." It refers to a clear, deliberate awareness of the movements of the inner processes that, in commonsense terms, we refer to as our "self." The more conscious and comfortable we are with the movements of these inner processes, the more peaceful and "in order" our experience of ourselves is. As we become more attentive to these inner processes, we begin to appreciate natural phases in how they move. We also discover that they are in a sense good—i.e., that they work well, and they lead us toward happiness and away from suffering. Even when "mistakes" are made, the patterns of these inner processes are self-correcting.

As we become more trusting of these inner processes and the natural phases they move through, we become more comfortable with releasing the commonsense view that there is a kind of fixed essence inside of us (a "self") who is somehow making all of these inner processes happen. Instead we recognize simply that they are processes unfolding, and these processes do follow natural patterns, and all of this is good and trustworthy. But they are not a "self," as such. There is no little mastermind within us that is responsible for all of this. We use the word "self" as a place-holding label for this inner world of processes, but the "self" as such is not more than that label. In the same way, we use the word "carpet" as a commonsense convention: a label to describe colored threads interwoven in a certain pattern onto a semi-firm backing. But if we pay closer attention, we notice that there really is no actual "carpet." There are threads and fabric dye and backing and glue and tacks. And if we attend more fully—which is to say less conceptually and more directly—we notice that the threads of thoughts and processes are made up of continually fluctuating processes, which are, in the end, simply emerging out of emptiness (*shunyata*) and returning back to it. So it is with the commonsense label "self."

The less conscious we are of the inner workings of these processes in our lives and their trustworthiness, the more frightening it is to hear that they are not a self in charge, in control of our lives. On the other hand, the more conscious we become of these processes and their trustworthiness, the more liberating it is to realize that a "self" is really not our true nature at all. When correctly understood (which includes direct awareness of these inner processes), there is nothing dehumanizing about not being a "self." Ironically, it is precisely through realizing that we are not some kind of master controller that we can come to a peaceful sense of self-possession, a sense of our lives being under control and in one piece.

An important meditative practice for the cultivation of wisdom and virtue in Buddhist training is to reflect on the movements of these inner processes and their patterns. This is the focus of this section: the truth of the eightfold path.

As a concrete example, let's say that the city of Ottawa represents being spiritually "awake," and the city of Windsor represents being spiritually "asleep." If I want to take the highway to Ottawa, it would be very helpful if the various signs along that stretch of the highway were mapped out for me as a guide (e.g., "right understanding," "right intention," "right action," etc.). It might also be helpful, in order to avoid ending up in Windsor, to know the various signs along that section of the highway, so that I could be quickly aware when I was off course (e.g. "wrong understanding," "wrong intention," "wrong action," etc.). But even more basic than any of this would be to understand what a highway is in the first place, and how to travel on one. In the same way, the Buddhist Path is built on a certain basic understanding of what it means to be a human being, whatever path in life we may choose to follow. That basic understanding involves what I am calling the eight processes of personal agency. A key distinctive of the Buddhist view, however, is that there is no mastermind, no self, no "agent" behind the processes of personal agency.

All of the terms in the triangle diagram below will gradually be defined, but here is a brief overview. The diagram shows eight phases in the process of being human that are continuously emerging from Being-As-Such.

Plants, non-human animals, and inanimate objects also emerge continuously from Being-As-Such. But only in human experience is there a real possibility of becoming conscious of the

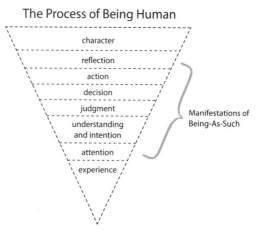

The Process of Being Human

character
reflection
action
decision
judgment
understanding
and intention
attention
experience

Manifestations of
Being-As-Such

Being-As-Such

transcendental nature of the process itself and its origins in Being-As-Such. Still, there is no "guarantee" of this growth in consciousness just because one is born human. The more ordinary outcome is identification with the phases of the process, which prevents awareness of the process as a whole; Being-As-Such is not separate from the ordinary operations of the human mind (attending to experience, understanding, judging, deciding, etc.). And in this ultimate sense, there is no real difference between Being-As-Such and any concrete human being. However, the nature and origin of these operations of the mind can be completely unknown when they are taken to be the expressions of an autonomous entity we call the "self."

The spiritual path is about becoming conscious of the process of personal agency as a whole and its harmony with Being-As-Such. We are on a journey to reach Being-As-Such, but we proceed on this journey not by *leaving* the processes of personal agency, but by becoming more *fully aware* of them, purifying them of illusion, so that we can better understand them as they are.

This is the paradox of "remaining" within human experience while "moving forward" spiritually.

Through spiritual practice, we are not transcending human experience, not transcending the processes of personal agency, but we transcend our *illusions* regarding those processes.

## Being-As-Such

Being-As-Such is a strange expression. I'm using it here to point out what is often called "suchness"—or *tathata*, in Pali. Being-As-Such is empty of identification with any of its manifestations. Not even the brahma viharas or the transcendent wisdom that understands the Four Noble Truths are inherent "contents" of Being-As-Such. They are, however, un-obscured manifestations of Being-As-Such. Being-As-Such is infinite openness, infinite freedom. Another way of expressing this is that Being-As-Such is "nondual"; it is beyond categories such as right/wrong, love/hate, sacred/secular, male/female, human/divine, etc. It is for this reason that the brahma viharas are described as a pure manifestation of Being-As-Such; they are not rooted in illusory dualistic conditions. They emerge from Being-As-Such and remain free of conditionality. Any quality that reflects such awareness of Being-As-Such is "transcendental"; it transcends the illusions of ordinary human existence regarding its true nature. It transcends the illusion that one is the ego, that one is the entity in charge of bodily sensations, thoughts, feelings, images, and so on. Being-As-Such is also described with terms such as "mind itself," or the "true nature of mind," or "Buddha nature," or just as "emptiness."

To reflect on duality and nonduality is difficult but important. These are not just obscure philosophical themes that have no relation to the practical quality of human life. Their relation to human development is not straightforward, however; it is subtle and paradoxical. Nondual awareness requires that one be objectively aware of duality, aware of it from the *outside* of it, without being enmeshed in it. And yet this awareness takes place in the *interior* world of experience; it is subjective. This relates to the insight of philosopher Bernard Lonergan that "objectivity is the fruit of authentic subjectivity." We come to see things as they truly are only when we are able to perceive duality as an object within consciousness, rather than as consciousness itself. It is like the difference between seeing the objective presence of a dusty lens, and seeing the entire world *through* that dusty lens, without being aware of the objective presence of that dusty lens. The former is authentic subjectivity, which is nondual and objective; the latter is a subjectivity that cannot perceive reality as it, because of the unrecognized constrictions imposed upon its horizon. At the same time, however, the dusty lens of duality appears to be necessary in human development. Without having been submerged in the perspective of duality, we would not be able to know the difference when we step out of duality, and to recognize duality itself as an object with which awareness was previously identified. Duality of subject and object is what all language and proto-language is predicated on. And in practical terms, this means that there is no awakening to nondual awareness without first having something like language, then becoming conscious of it as an object within interiority, so that identification with it can be transcended. We have to be critically conscious, aware of the label as an existent object within our interiority, rather than identifying it as "my" consciousness itself. Let's now turn our attention to each of the elements in the above diagram.

*Dependent Origination.* Between Being-As-Such and the manifestation of experience that we call "human beings," there is a space. In that space, a complex process happens, which the Buddha called "dependent origination." This process is rooted in ignorance, or lack of awareness, of Being-As-Such. In an important way, dependent origination is yet another, more microscopic, view of the process surrounding the dynamics of tanha. Ordinary human experience is a result of this process.

This means that ordinary human experience only arises from and is sustained through the illusion of duality, in which the true nature of Being-As-Such is falsely divided by the process of dependent origination into two divisions: that which is "I" and that which is "not I." This does not mean that human beings are an illusion. It means that we are not real in the way that we usually imagine ourselves to be—as separate, autonomous "I"s or beings, separable from the processes that arise in each moment.

In traditional Buddhist language, when we are fully awake, we stop being "born." Our consciousness is no longer caught in the illusions of dependent origination; we perceive our true nature in Being-As-Such; we are conscious that Being-As-Such is what we are. We still experience, understand, and intend, but we are fully conscious of these processes as manifestations of Being-As-Such. We also cease to "die," because only that which is "born" (caught in the illusions of dependent origination) can "die." This does not, of course, mean that we as human beings live forever. It means that our true nature was never born and never dies, and to the extent that we are aware of it, we were never born and we never die. Awakening to our true nature is not an all-or-nothing proposition. The more aware we become of our true nature, the less we suffer, because ignorance of our true nature is the ultimate cause of suffering.

***Experience and Attention.*** Attention refers to intentional aware-ness of human experience. Human experience refers to the sounds, sights, smells, tastes, and touch sensations of the five sense organs, combined with what the Buddha called the sixth "sense organ"—that aspect of mind which generates thoughts, emotions, images, and other mental phenomena. It's worth not-ing that this aspect of mind, the "thought generator," is regulated by character, where remembered versions of the past that are judged to contain valuable information are stored for future ref-erence. In the Tibetan tradition, this is referred to as the "small mind" (*sem*), in contrast to the "large mind" (*rigpa*), which is our true nature. It is probably very wise to have different words to dis-tinguish these two. The contemporary commonsense under-standing of the word mind is essentially that of the "small mind."

Experience plays a central role in Buddhist practice, yet, with-out attention, there is no awareness of experience. Attention is the base of all the meditative dimensions of the path—right effort, right mindfulness, and right absorption. When attention to expe-rience is partial, the understanding of the experience is also par-tial. Ordinary human experience is not "pure experience" as it emerges from Being-As-Such. Ordinary experience is highly modified into a "version" of pure experience.

***Understanding and Intention.*** The understanding of experience engages feelings, imagination, concepts, and reasoning in a process of inner discourse to determine what it is that is being experienced. Understanding and intention are linked in the Bud-dha's Dharma as the objective and subjective poles of wisdom. Because of this special relation, they are presented together in the triangle. Understanding of experience is always dynamically interacting with intention toward experience. For example: if the experience attended to is a sound that enters your room, the understanding might be "It is an absolutely delightful sound that fills my heart with joy and makes me realize that life is worth living" or "It is an obnoxious sound that ruins my entire day and should be against the law" or perhaps something in between. Intentions and subsequent reactions toward the sound (e.g. of clinging or aversion) would be shaped by these different understandings and also influence those understandings. The commonsense view is that to enjoy something pleasant involves clinging to it, just as to protect oneself from something painful is viewed as involving aversion toward it. The Path opens up the possibility of a middle way of relating that is more liberating, because it is able to enjoy and self-protect without the dynamics of clinging or aversion, which produce suffering.

To appreciate the constant interconnectedness of understanding and intention, it might be helpful to also talk about these two processes with just one word, such as "values." We can think of values as intentions that are rooted in particular understandings of the *good,* the *bad,* and the *neutral.* These make up three classes of values that we hold—positive values, negative values, and neutral values. Positive values are deeply held perceptions (as opposed to beliefs, which we may not consider practical, or opinions, which may be relative or changeable) of "the good," i.e., the true sources of well-being. Negative values are actual perceptions of "the bad," i.e., the true sources of suffering. Neutral values are actual perceptions of "neither-good-nor-bad," i.e. a true source of neither well-being nor suffering. In all values there is an understanding that truth has been found, together with an aim to realize that truth. This does not mean that any given value relates to a *correct* understanding. For example, a judge may accept a bribe to set free a wealthy person who is actually guilty

of a crime and to imprison a poor person who is actually inno-
cent in his place. That judge's action reflects a positive value
regarding money (that it is a "true" source of well-being), a negative value regarding doing the right thing when it's not prof-
itable, and a neutral value regarding unjust imprisonment. The
judge's actions confirm that these are his actual perceptions of
what is true, although he may have different surface opinions or
beliefs about what is good, bad, and neutral in such a situation.
The judge's actions, in reality, are harmful to all parties involved,
including himself. But the point here is that his actual values, the
actual understandings and intentions that are governing his perceptions (and which are likely embedded in his historical character), tell him that he is pursuing a true source of well-being.
Otherwise, he would not pursue it. We desire to possess what
our values perceive as good, we desire to eliminate what our values perceive as bad, and we desire to ignore what our values perceive as neutral. And so the accuracy of the understandings that
feed our intentions is key. They will influence how we pay attention, what we decide "counts" as a valuable experience in our
perception.

*Judgment.* Judgment is a process of sorting through feelings and
other evidence that are supporting a particular understanding of
experience, and seeking to determine whether the understanding
is true. In the Buddhist tradition, a critical aspect of judgment is
detecting the presence of suffering within the active understanding and intention. Suffering is experiential evidence that the
understanding and intention are clouded by illusion. Another
critical aspect of judgment is determining whether or not this
particular understanding is supported by "the wise." The "wise"
are not simply persons in authority, but persons whose lives show

actual evidence of happiness, compassion, self-awareness, virtue, and other such traits we value.

For example, the standard of truth adopted in Buddhist practice is the Four Noble Truths, but these are not adopted as "absolutes" that are always true no matter what. Their truth is always relative to their actual capacity to bring suffering to an end. And so, in Buddhist practice, the Four Noble Truths are constantly being tested; our understanding of them is being constantly refined based on actual experience. These truths are dynamic rather than static. This ongoing process of judgment is reflected in the meditation symbol of "the Silent Watcher," who identifies and relinquishes false understandings of experience, and affirms and strengthens true understandings of experience. The Silent Watcher is the "one" that knows how these four truths relate to whatever is happening now. It is important to note, however, that even this Silent Watcher is ultimately empty in the same way the apparent "self" is.

Many meditators find it very challenging to bring meditative awareness into their everyday life experience. When we struggle with this problem of integration, it can be helpful to remember that meditative awareness is in fact a process of judgment, a process of determining the truth of a particular understanding of experience. It functions identically inside and outside of formal meditation practice. And it is the very same judgment process that is involved in meditative awareness that is also involved in ethical practice and wisdom practice.

**Decision.** An understanding of an experience may be true but still not necessarily good to act on in a particular moment or context. Also, there are many different ways that you can act on a particular understanding, not all of which may be good in the particular situation. Decision explores these kinds of basic questions: "What is the best way to act on this understanding?" and "Is it best to act on here and now, or in another context?" Decision focuses on preventing harmful consequences and fostering helpful ones by widening the net of attention prior to taking action. Notice that such a focus in decision-making itself depends on active understandings, intentions, and judgments.

*Action.* Action refers to purposive physical or mental movements toward the end decided upon through the process of attending/understanding/intending/judging/deciding. Part of walking the path is the commitment to let certain vows guide one's actions; this helps to create a "buffer zone" of contemplative space prior to action (we'll explore this more in the next chapter). Here, suffice it to say that this facilitates clearer awareness of the processes of attention, understanding, intention, judgment, and decision. Meditation training provides the inner calm and the friendly sensitivity to subtle processes that are necessary to make use of this buffer zone. Wisdom training (such as the one you are engaged in now by studying Dharma) provides the larger philosophical framework that helps us keep track of the big picture of what and how and why we are practicing. Perhaps Buddhism's greatest contribution to the understanding of human action is its integral view, which includes not only the whole person, but also all others and Being-As-Such.

*Reflection.* Reflection refers to the process of understanding actions, both in terms of their antecedents and their consequences, with a focus on the experience of suffering and flourishing in our lives. Reflection is critically important because it is not always possible for us to arrive at accurate understandings of our experience before we act. It is sometimes only through careful reflection on the consequences of past actions that we come to see the false understandings and intentions that were informing them; as they say, "hindsight is 20/20." Clarifying reflection is the purpose of all wisdom practices. Study of the Dharma is never an end in itself. Wisdom remains conceptual until reflection discovers the interior realities it is pertinent to. If wisdom remains only conceptual, it may be interesting, but it is not yet Dharma.

*Historical Character.* Character is the particular disposition to attend, understand, intend, judge, decide, act, and reflect that (for better or worse) has evolved out of the history of a person. It is a kind of summary of the process of being human, as we have experienced it from birth onward. It reflects the kind of person that we appear to be most of the time. It is not only individual persons that have such a character; larger bodies such as families, neighborhoods, towns, and nations also have their own characters. And all individual persons are part of these larger bodies, just as cells are part of tissues, and tissues make up organs, and organs make up organisms. Because of the interdependent quality of his or her true nature, this is true of every individual person even if he/she is a hermit who remains in solitude. Traditionally, the ego—the illusion that one is one's character—is the continuing factor that moves on from one life to the next, being continually reborn until it is fully overcome and all that remains is Being-As-Such.

Being-As-Such is dynamic, always moving in the direction of flourishing. Character is more static and rule-based, always suggesting movement in the direction that seemed best yesterday. The great challenge of spiritual practice is that even if yesterday's understandings, intentions, judgments, decisions, and actions were truly best, that was yesterday. The entire process is moving anew today. This is not to say that character is not helpful. At times it is our best counsel. But even the character of a buddha—however wonderful it may be—is a relic, a thing of the past, not a dispenser of eternal truth. A wise character is one that has made turning toward process, which is rooted in Being-As-Such, its basic rule.

In my experience, there are some pieces of character which are so taken for granted as oneself, as eternal, as absolutely true in their view of well-being and its causes that they only become conscious in response to life vicissitudes that are of crisis intensity, when panic sets in over one of character's big rules being broken. In such moments, we feel the power of character; it really does seem as though there is an autonomous entity inside of us that has taken control of our cognitive operations, perhaps even against our better judgment. After we have experienced this a few times, though, we seem to be quicker to recognize what is happening within us. But even then, it seems to take considerable time to work through these kinds of challenges to the major rules of character, which, after all, were not built up overnight.

Whatever the specific form of a character is, its basic function remains the same. Based on memories of past successes and failures, character informs all of the prior seven phases in the process of being human: instructing us to attend to what it deems is important, to understand which view is best to take, to judge the truth of our understanding, to decide on the best course of action, and to reflect on our actions and their consequences.

# CHAPTER SIX

# Dependent Origination, Personal Agency, and the Silent Watcher

## *Dependent Origination and Personal Agency*

From here on in the readings, I will use the term "personal agency" to mean "the natural movement of the processes of attending, understanding, intending, judging, deciding, acting, reflecting, and remembering." The less constricted and the more sustained the awareness is of these eight processes, the greater awareness of personal agency one has. Although Buddhism affirms all of the details of the process of personal agency, it also teaches that there is no "agent," no "self," behind the scenes directing the process. The concept of an agent or self who manages the process is tacked on to what is actually happening, in order to explain and control what is happening. But, we may wonder, *who* needs to explain and control what is happening? The short answer is that the brain does, in order to ensure the survival of the organism. And, paradoxically, having a brain that is capable of fooling itself, capable of creating the illusion of self, seems to be necessary for the spiritual development of personal agency.

Before we get into the details of the path in the next chapter, we will explore these workings of dependent origination a bit further, so that we can better appreciate how the path both unveils these workings and enables awareness of that which is beneath them, that which is deeper than the conditioned, phenomenal level of reality, and is the true nature of sentient being.

The traditional teaching of dependent origination of all phenomena involves twelve complex links, which I will summarize here, in terms of three phases—early, middle, and late phases. The traditional teaching also relates to all temporal reality (humans, animals, rocks, trees, etc.), but this three-phase interpretation is explained in a way that is limited to human beings, which makes it easier to understand intuitively.

The Zen Buddhist teacher Kitaro Nishida uses the term "pure experience" to describe reality that has not been "processed" by dependent origination. I will use that same term here with the same meaning. When pure experience has been modified by dependent origination, I will call that "egoic" experience, because it divides up all reality into the either/or categories of "I" and "not I." Instead of continuing to use the strange term "not I," I will use the term "Other," with a capital "O," to signify everything within the field of dualistic perception that is *not* the ego. So, when you see the word "Other" with a capital "O" it may refer to a person, or a stick, or a car, or literally anything that is perceived as Other than the ego.

In the initial modifications of pure experience by dependent origination, a feeling of pleasure may be understood as an "I" experience, while a feeling of pain, or a visual image of a tree or a rock may be understood as an "Other" or "not I" experience. At this level of consciousness, the many "I" experiences are not integrated into a cohesive whole. Similarly, the many "not I" or "Other" experiences are not organized into larger categories (such as "living," "not living," "young," "old," "animal," "vegetable," "mineral," and so on.) And, also, there are no meaningful relationships spelled out between the "I" experiences and the "Other" experiences (such as "when I *sit under this* tree I feel relaxed").

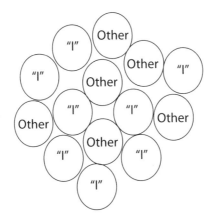

Early Phases of Dependent Origination

As a result this level of experience may be felt as chaotic. It is probably how infants experience themselves and the world, and how we also may experience life when we are in crisis, or at certain points in the process of meditation.

This chaotic experience gets organized further through processes of sorting and identification as we navigate through life experiences. Certain "I" experiences are identified with and become consolidated into one more or less coherent experience of who I am (the ego).

This allows "not I" or "Other" experiences to be further organized by thought into groups, according to the various concerns of the individual ego.

These organizations are held intact by the forming and

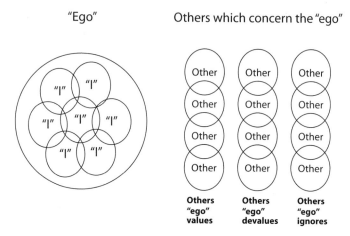

"Ego"          Others which concern the "ego"

| Other | Other | Other |
| Other | Other | Other |
| Other | Other | Other |
| Other | Other | Other |

| Others "ego" values | Others "ego" devalues | Others "ego" ignores |

Middle Phases of Dependent Origination

strengthening of emotional bonds ("attachments") between the ego and the Others that concern it. These bonds serve the function of ensuring the survival of the individual ego. This octopus-like structure depicts fully developed egoic consciousness. In earlier chapters, this same condition was described in terms of the

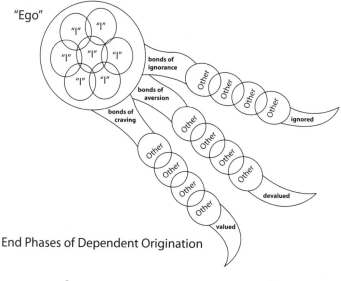

End Phases of Dependent Origination

myth of the yogis and the fantasy of samsara—and explained as being the ultimate cause of human suffering (chapter 3).

The purpose of the three trainings of Buddhist practice, which make up the path, is to cultivate experiential insight into this modified, egoic experience, so that it may be transcended, enabling greater awareness of pure experience and the processes of personal agency. The purpose of the path is thus to become increasingly conscious of the workings of dependent origination and their distortions of pure experience and the processes of personal agency.

As we've discussed, experiential insight into the workings of tanha interrupts the mechanics of dependent origination, and with that its obscurations cease and the true nature of the mind

**The functioning of dependent origination**

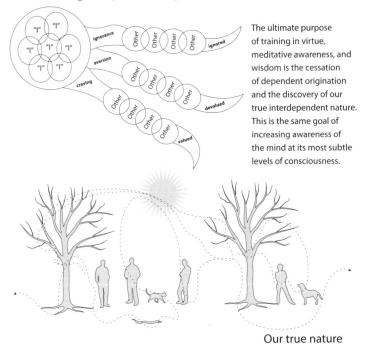

The ultimate purpose of training in virtue, meditative awareness, and wisdom is the cessation of dependent origination and the discovery of our true interdependent nature. This is the same goal of increasing awareness of the mind at its most subtle levels of consciousness.

Our true nature

becomes apparent. The bonds of clinging, aversion, and ignorance, which attach the ego to the Others that concern it, simulate or mimic the actual interdependent nature of all life, in which everything is recognized as a *Thou* whose well-being is cherished, including one's own life.

## The Silent Watcher

As introduced earlier, the Silent Watcher is a symbolic figure (as opposed to a literal one) who relates with wisdom and compassion to everything that is. The Silent Watcher is often used as a symbol of meditative awareness.

The Thai Buddhist monk Ajahn Chah used to say to the students in his forest monastery: "Try to be mindful, and let things take their natural course. Then your mind will become still in any surroundings, like a clear forest pool. All kinds of wonderful rare animals will come to drink at the pool, and you will clearly see the nature of all things. You will see many strange and wonderful things come and go, but you will be still. This is the happiness of the Buddha." This Silent Watcher is in fact a symbol of that level of consciousness called *buddha*.

The heart of meditative awareness is expressed well in this symbol of a Silent Watcher, who simply attends very fully to what comes and what goes, with a kind, non-intrusive interest. She does not seek to influence what she sees, but wants very simply and respectfully to know it, as fully as possible, as it is. She is like the wise elder, sitting silently and still at the edge of a pond in the middle of a forest. As she sits, she observes the different animals that come out of the forest to the pond to drink. She observes the small animals. She observes the large animals. The beautiful ones. The ugly ones. The quiet and the loud ones. She does not really mind which animal comes and which animal goes. All she wants is to experience what freely emerges from the forest as it is. She does not cling to the beautiful ones. She does not fear the large ones. She does not ignore the small ones. She simply watches each arrival with a friendly and unobtrusive interest, getting to know it as it is, until it returns to the forest. She relates to these visitors with such a lightness and kindness of heart that they relax in her presence and show her their true nature.

This is the practice of meditative awareness. The Silent Watcher is a symbol of the way of seeing that is meditative awareness. This awareness observes the uninterrupted stream of thoughts, images, feelings, and sensations, which arise and return from whence they came, moment by moment. Whether they arise slowly, one at a time, or in rapid succession, it watches them with the same kind, unobtrusive interest. It notices thoughts and feelings as they arise. It notices images and physical sensations as they arise. It observes their characteristics. If they are unpleasant, it observes the unpleasantness, without trying to make it "go away." If they are pleasant, it observes the pleasure, without trying to prolong its stay. If they are neutral, it observes them anyway, with the same presence of mind, not diminishing their importance or ignoring them. It watches them all, arising, staying for a while, and returning from whence they came. With training in the development of such meditative awareness, we discover the cessation of the afflictive emotions of willed ignorance, greed, and hatred, and their related fears and anxieties. In turn, we discover the greater accessibility of wholesome states of mind, such as goodwill, compassion, equanimity, and joy in the happiness of others—the brahma viharas.

As the Silent Watcher allows experience to unfold, continually letting go of identifications for the sake of being fully present to whatever is arising, there is a movement of consciousness into its depths, into its origins, into Being-As-Such. The Silent Watcher attends, understands, intends, judges, decides, acts, reflects, and remembers with a mind that is aware of its origins in the pure experience of Being-As-Such. Because of this, the relational bonds that connect all of reality are perceived. These bonds transcend the duality of ego and Other, and the associated attachments of clinging, aversion, and ignorance. The nature of these transcendental bonds are the brahma viharas, the intentions that manifest out of a clear awareness of Being-As-Such in relation to whatever is arising. In the shorthand terms of the eightfold path, which will be discussed below, this is described as the mutual influence of "right understanding" and "right intention" on one another.

The process in the mind that the Silent Watcher points to, however, is not the ultimate reality of Being-As-Such; it is still an impermanent manifestation, a *sign of* Being-As-Such. But it is a valid sign that the reality of Being-As-Such is "close," in the same way that smoke is a valid sign that fire is close. The form of the Silent Watcher embodies the brahma viharas, which are direct, unobscured manifestations of Being-As-Such. When one encounters the level of mind represented by the Silent Watcher, that process becomes a portal into awareness of Being-As-Such. And the form of the Silent Watcher dissolves into the formlessness of Being-As-Such.

The bottom line, psychologically, is that through practicing the Path we can be experientially liberated from the narcissistic circle that ordinarily regulates our consciousness, and thereby generates suffering within ourselves, others, and the world.

# CHAPTER SEVEN

# The Path as Spiritual Discipline

## *The Value of Summary*

In a nutshell, the truth of the path teaches us that "When we silently listen to the truth of our lives and the lives of others, we do good, and we flourish. And when at times we cannot hear that truth, if we still do good, according to our best understanding, we still flourish, only not as profoundly." In practice, those two sentences are how I understand and follow the Path in my life most of the time. Reflecting on the Buddha's teachings has influenced how I understand words like "listen," "truth," "good," and "flourish," but even still, it is quite a simple way of living. For me it has been essential to have a simple, "nutshell" understanding of the path that comes from my own experience of what Buddhist training is like for me. Sometimes "holding on" is a very good thing to do. Having that simple, personalized framework to hold on to seems to allow me to reflect more freely and deeply on the complexities of the path. And those reflections nourish and deepen my experiential, "nutshell" understanding of what it means to live the spiritual life. My teacher in Sri Lanka summarized the path in his experience with "Inner peace is outer peace." I found that inspiring, and it obviously had deep significance for my teacher, but it wasn't quite enough for me. So I had to create my own understanding, based on how I experience meditating, practicing virtue in my relationships with others, and reflecting on the Four Noble Truths. This kind of experiential summarizing is something that we tend to do anyway, but not always consciously and explicitly. It has been very helpful in my practice to do it consciously and explicitly.

Honoring our inner, experiential understandings of the spiritual life is, in itself, a very important teaching. To a certain extent, before we ever read a book or hear a talk about the path, we already understand it intuitively. As we formally study the Dharma, we discover that the reason this is so is because the path is not something external to us; it is built in to who we are. And we have been exploring it long before we first encountered the teachings of the Buddha. When we consciously put into words our intuitive understandings of the spiritual life, we are mining for the nuggets of Dharma that we have already discovered in life. We may have discovered them through difficult life circumstances, through religious or artistic experiences, through psychotherapy or other relationships, or just through the unique journey of living our lives. Our lives always reveal our present understanding of the path, at each stage of development.

So before reading the rest of this chapter, I'd like to encourage you to take some time to put into words your own intuitive understanding of the spiritual life, based on your own lived experience. Don't get carried away. Just reflect inwardly for a while and write down a sentence or two about the spiritual life that, based on your experience, you feel is so true and liberating that you tend to actually live by it (i.e. it's not just a platitude). Enjoy it. Reflect on how the living of your life has revealed it to you. At the same time, hold on to it lightly. Be open to understanding it more deeply than you do right now, and be open to its evolution in directions that you cannot predict right now.

## The Role of Discipline

The blissful, virtuous consciousness of nirodha is unconditioned; it does not require discipline to sustain itself. And yet, experiencing that level of consciousness involves certain sensitivities, which can be cultivated. Discipline plays a role in cultivating all of the conditioned aspects of existence that are required for our flourishing as human beings—such as caring for our bodies, allotting time for meditation and study, learning skillful ways to communicate and act in relation to others, and so on. These are things that require development, and they only develop well when the right conditions and experiences are in place. For example, if I never leave my desk during the day, I will likely not develop a daily routine of physical exercise. Similarly, unless I make a conscious effort to block out time for formal meditation (and actually show up on time), I will likely not develop a daily meditation practice.

Discipline is a very mundane thing. It involves planning and organizing, decision-making, and the establishing of rituals that organize one's life. Often we are encouraged to endure discipline's unpleasant aspects by focusing on the long-term payoffs that will result. This can help to assure us that we are not in fact being foolish, but wise, because in the end we will enjoy even greater pleasure than would have been possible without the sacrifice. Examples of this kind of thinking range from the promise that we will grow up to be strong if we eat our spinach, to the promise that we will go to heaven when we die if we follow certain challenging rules here on earth. The formula is used often, because it often works. And there is some underlying wisdom in it. In health, we engage in discipline in order to flourish.

Training does require motivation, and the lure of positive results such as increased self-awareness, decreased stress, improved relationships, and so on can be a helpful motivator in those moments when we don't particularly feel like doing our developmental or spiritual work. And yet the egoic mind often resists. The habits cultivated on the path can pose a threat to the ego's domination of consciousness, and one way to reduce that threat is for the ego to simply encourage us to not engage in the trainings. For example, it is quite amazing how motivation for other things, like dusting or shopping or going for a walk, can suddenly grow when our scheduled meditation time is approaching.

At a deeper level, discipline involves an emotional sacrifice of giving time and energy to some process that, like life itself, does not always offer pleasure. And because we know that life, on its own, will bring us much that is unpleasant, it can seem foolish to actually choose an activity that brings us into closer contact with things that we do not like to experience. Especially in our free time, we might rather choose activities that have some guarantee of "pleasure only."

Beginning the disciplines of contemplative living can sometimes feel like finding oneself undertaking the care of a small child and feeling unprepared for what it might involve. It is often quite surprising to discover the different fears and fantasies that can arise and begin to inhibit commitment to contemplative disciplines. Talking about these challenges with others who are also engaging in the same process can be very helpful, much like a parenting support group can be for new parents.

For some people, discipline is associated with having to submit to moralistic authorities (either internal or external or both), authorities that may not be either aware of or concerned about the person's well-being. And in such contexts, we can learn to oppose discipline in general. For others, there can be an erotic-like attraction to discipline, which often leads to overzealous and harsh treatment of "undisciplined" aspects of oneself. Both of these patterns create a self-defeating trap that can be very hard to get out of. In such situations, the unhealthy meanings and purposes underlying the discipline need to be addressed so that discipline can be consciously re-appropriated as a healthy means of securing benefit for oneself and others. Unlike the root problem of egoic consciousness, these types of difficulty can be effectively dealt with in traditional counseling or psychotherapy.

Over time, as we experience the benefits of the path, discipline becomes less of a pressing issue. We develop skillful habits. We are encouraged by friends in our spiritual community. We also come to directly understand the relationship between our flourishing and our practicing. And, at a deeper level, "right intention" itself increasingly becomes the motivation for spiritual training.

Yet in the beginning, in the experience of everyone I have ever known, there always seems to be certain moments when it is only the pleasure of imagining a future benefit that can get us back into training in the present moment. And this is not a problem—in fact, the Buddha consciously used this approach when necessary to help motivate his students.

## Working with Resistance

The experience of "resistance" to the practice of spiritual disciplines that make up the path is a place of great potential insight into the first three truths of the Buddha's Dharma. In my experience it has been very helpful to approach this resistance simply with a desire to understand it, rather than with a view to "overcoming" it. The disciplines of the path definitely initiate the kind of creative dis-illusionment, or brokenness, which softens the heart and ushers in transcendent awareness and insight. Fear of the unknown consequences of this loss can be very powerful. Some form of this fear is what we often discover when we explore our resistance to a discipline of the path. It is all too easy to explain these reactions away with quick identifications such as "I'm just lazy," or to try arm-wrestling them into strict compliance. Neither approach ultimately does any good; on the contrary, they weaken our spontaneous motivation. Gentle, patient exploration, on the other hand, can yield powerful insights that actually dissolve the resistance. Resistances, just like all phenomena that we hope to understand, need to be approached with acceptance, respect, and genuine interest.

It's important to recognize that experiencing resistance to spiritual discipline is not a "bad" thing, to be conquered and eliminated. Neither is it something to be ignored. It is an integral, predictable part of the process. When there is strong attachment to a particular story in the mind about who we and others are, there is naturally going to be resistance to the dis-illusionment process. Carefully, respectfully exploring it is itself following the path.

## Wise Resistances

In some contexts, resistances to spiritual discipline are not primarily about resisting the breaking of an inner attachment. If our basic physical needs are not met, or if we lack supportive, virtuous relationships—the support of community—resistance to spiritual disciplines may have a broader significance. In fact, it cannot be fully resolved without correcting the basic material and/or social deficits that are conditioning it. Resistance in such a case is better understood as a kind of alarm, the sounding of which signifies that one is not yet in a position to deeply engage in spiritual disciplines. Resistances of this type might be best thought of as "wise resistances." Indeed, the Buddha once found himself in such a position due to malnutrition, and was only able to resume formal spiritual practices after an extensive period of rehabilitation, in which he was nursed back to health by a kind stranger.

There are many varieties of malnutrition, some of the most harmful of which are social in nature. One of the Buddha's disciples, a woman named Kisa Gotami, initially came to him in essentially what modern psychology might describe as a postpartum psychosis—carrying her dead infant and demanding the Buddha bring the child back to life. Her life was riddled with destructive sociopsychological dynamics, including a very cruel marital and family situation. She had been so marginalized that she no longer had a feeling of common humanity with other people. She was in no position to reflect on the shared meanings, or to take up the spiritual disciplines, which united the Buddha's community. And so, the Buddha offered a unique social intervention for her: He asked her to bring him a mustard seed from the home of a family that had not known a similar loss. In attempting to do this, she normalized her experience of herself in the local community, and this enabled her to finally grieve for her son and her many other losses. Once these most basic needs were addressed, her life stabilized, and she returned to the Buddha, now able to pursue a deeper level of spiritual development—and asked for the

Dharma. Eventually she chose to ordain and, as an elder nun, was recognized as a prominent poet in the spiritual community.

It is important to note that the Buddha not only helped Kisa to recover from her crisis, he also provided her with a safe place to live and grow—a spiritual community where, as a divorced woman of lower caste, she would not only be accepted, cared for, and taught, but she could also achieve a position of great honor. It is also important to note that, in this process, Kisa's image of herself as an empty, unworthy, outcast—an image to which she was deeply attached—was broken, and that the support and the guidance of the spiritual community provided her with a context where she was able to experience this brokenness that liberates the heart and opens up a deeper, freer sense of identity. Her poetry in the scriptural text called *Verses of the Elder Nuns* suggests that, during her years in the spiritual community, she must have encountered many more subtle, more difficult, and less wise forms of resistance to spiritual discipline, as she faced the narrative legacy in her mind of the many traumatic social interactions that she had experienced in her youth. It is unlikely that her life would have flourished as it did if the Buddha had only taught her a few spiritual disciplines and then sent her back into the destructive social context that she had come out of. In that case, the resistances she would have faced would likely have been insurmountable.

Her story illustrates what an essential resource a healthy spiritual community can be for us as we attempt to follow the spiritual path. It also highlights the extraordinary potential that can be present in persons who, on the surface, may appear to be completely beyond hope.

# CHAPTER EIGHT

# The Eight Disciplines of the Path

The path is made up of eight interconnected spiritual disciplines: right understanding, right intention, right (internal) effort, right mindfulness (attentiveness), right mental absorption, right speech, right action, and right livelihood. The Pali word *samma,* traditionally translated into English as "right," could also be translated as "best," or "pure." Each path dimension is contrasted with its opposite—wrong understanding, wrong intention, wrong speech, etc. For example, right understanding involves comprehending life experience in terms of the Four Noble Truths, while wrong understanding fails to see the cause of dukkha in tanha and its cessation in nirodha. The eight disciplines of the path are often visualized as spokes on a wheel, called the *dharmachakra.*

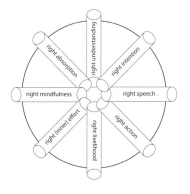

These eight dimensions of the path do not map onto the eight processes of personal agency in a one-to-one fashion. Rather all of the eight processes of personal agency are present within each dimension of the path. Each dimension of the path requires awareness of every process of personal agency. In practice, our understanding of the path often seems to be focused on only one or a few aspects of personal agency. For example, when we are impressed in our meditation practice by the impact of having more full attention, we may naturally feel that the path is "all about attention." We will start to view difficult situations in our lives and the lives of others as problems related to constricted attention. We may start to view our more favorable experiences in terms of more full attention. Or, when we are studying the first and second noble truths, we may be impressed by how influential on our lives our understanding of the causes of suffering is. We may come to see the roots of all problems in false understandings of the causes of suffering, and come to view the path as "all about understanding." There is certainly truth in these impressions, and sometimes we learn by focusing on one thing as though it were all that mattered. In reality, though, the path is not "all about" any one process of personal agency, but about personal agency as a whole. Indeed, the path itself is all about everything in human experience. This is important to keep in mind or our understanding and practice of the path can become imbalanced.

One way that the path maintains balance is by engaging us in three different types of training simultaneously. Engaging in less than the full three trainings promotes imbalance. The eight practice dimensions are divided up into three trainings as pictured on the next page.

These groupings, like the four truths themselves, were not arbitrary or simply logical, but also related to different levels of

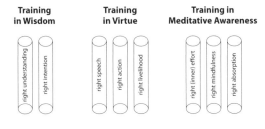

Fourth Noble Truth
(= the eightfold path)
(= the three trainings)

| Training in Wisdom | Training in Virtue | Training in Meditative Awareness |
|---|---|---|
| right understanding · right intention | right speech · right action · right livelihood | right (inner) effort · right mindfulness · right absorption |

*The three trainings*

consciousness. The virtue group focuses on the gross level of consciousness, as it manifests in objective actions, speech, and livelihood/vocation (how time is occupied). The meditative group focuses on the more subtle level of consciousness of our inner world, which is wholly subjective. The wisdom group focuses on the very subtle level of consciousness, which makes up the horizon of the perceptible—that which is possible for us to experience, both subjectively and objectively.

Like an iceberg in the ocean, consciousness is unitary, but it is not necessarily apparent in its entirety. The "water level" for some persons may be very low; they are able to perceive very subtle levels of the mind. Others may not be able to perceive below the gross level of their actions. Also, we may be deeply perceptive in some contexts—such as in crisis, or in solitude, or in the midst of nature—but remain quite superficially perceptive in others, such as at work or at the supermarket. And all of this variation has implications for how we will engage with the different aspects of Buddhist training. In general, the more of consciousness that can be engaged in the training process, the better. And the trainings themselves foster this integration between different levels of consciousness.

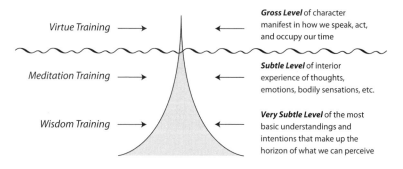

Virtue Training →  ← **Gross Level** of character manifest in how we speak, act, and occupy our time

Meditation Training →  ← **Subtle Level** of interior experience of thoughts, emotions, bodily sensations, etc.

Wisdom Training →  ← **Very Subtle Level** of the most basic understandings and intentions that make up the horizon of what we can perceive

*The full functioning of the path is not always apparent.*

There are countless stories of spiritual seekers who seem to be constantly meditating, but their interactions with other people overflow with conflict and tension. Others may focus intensely on concrete lifestyle issues but have little awareness of their emotional lives. Still others may be happily engrossed in the careful study of philosophical texts, but be quite averse to engaging in the more imprecise and messy worlds of interiority and interpersonal interaction. The Buddha's Middle Way encourages a more well-rounded and humble approach based on balance and integration. It does not neglect one dimension of consciousness in favor of another. Instead it purposefully maintains balance and integration within the mind.

In addition to assuring breadth and balance in our practice of the path as a whole, we also attend to our level of practice within each of the eight path dimensions.

## The Path as Crucible

Together, the eight spiritual disciplines make up a comprehensive path for human development. A central metaphor used by the

Buddha for this developmental process was that it was a process of purification. Together, the eight spiritual disciplines, by focusing awareness on the reality of the present moment, form a crucible for the evolution of consciousness toward pure experience. A crucible is a special kind of container made out of a very durable heat-resistant material, so that it will withstand high temperatures. Because the container itself will not leak or melt down, it can be safely used to heat up precious metals, such as gold ore, to the point that the ore melts. Then, because of the high temperatures of the process, many of the impurities in the gold evaporate. The more dense impurities that don't evaporate into the air rise to the top of the liquid gold, where they can be manually skimmed off by the goldsmith. So that, in the end, all that remains is pure gold.

As we walk the spiritual path, the present moment is the crucible in which the eight disciplines provide the heat that purify our consciousness, leaving only the indestructible nature of mind itself. Each of the eight disciplines fosters understanding in

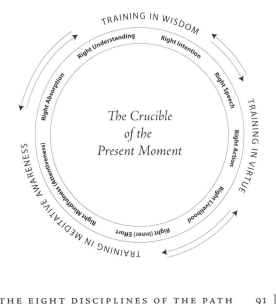

everyday life of the first three noble truths—dukkha, tanha, and nirodha. In each of the eight disciplines, we take the same basic journey out of dukkha, through a right understanding and response to tanha, into the liberation of nirodha. Because each discipline draws on a unique domain of consciousness, each also has its own unique shape and characteristics. They fit together, however, to form a solid crucible of training. Safely contained by this crucible, we evolve spiritually and discover the mind's true nature.

# CHAPTER NINE

# The Primacy of Wisdom and the Root of Virtue

There is one sense in which the eight disciplines are not equal in importance. Wisdom about the journey, reflected in right understanding and right intention, is what infuses and informs the other six disciplines. This highlights the importance of understanding the journey outlined in the first three truths before taking up the path. By engaging in the disciplines of the path as a whole, we thus end up devoting a great deal of time within our everyday experiences to training in wisdom, because the trainings in both virtue and meditative awareness incorporate the disciplines of wisdom.

It might be better for some of us to begin at the gross level of character, focusing on our overt actions, the things we say, and how we occupy our time. Or perhaps, for others, focusing on our inner lives through meditation training might be a more natural starting point. There is no hard and fast rule in Buddhism as to where and how to begin exploring the Dharma. The Buddha's general perspective, though, was that the broader a person's initial philosophical horizon is, the better he or she will be able to understand, and productively engage in, the other trainings of the path. For example, a person who understands his suffering solely in terms of external causes would likely not see enough value in practices like virtue training or meditation training to explore them in the first place. A person, on the other hand, who is less rigidly certain about her identity and the nature of life, would likely be more open to exploring her character and the subtleties of her inner life.

In another sense, because the gross, the subtle, and the very subtle levels of consciousness are all interconnected, it really doesn't matter where one begins. For example, the Buddha would often initially suggest a virtue training, like practicing generosity, to would-be disciples. Of course, not everyone would be interested in engaging in this kind of practice. But to those who were and did, he would then teach a little more. Then, if they could engage with that further teaching, he would add a little more, and a little more, until he reached the pièce de résistance of the four truths. At any point in the process, people could, and did, drop out. This approach might seem prejudicial or undemocratic, in that not everyone gets to learn the "whole package" of what he had to say about the art of living. But for the Buddha, this gradual approach was a very important teaching strategy. He did not want to force people to go where they were not ready or willing or prepared to go. This approach also had to do with respecting the truths that he had discovered by not putting them forward indiscriminately, in contexts where they would likely be misconstrued and thus risk creating more harm than good. This naturally made his spiritual community a safer place to learn the art of living.

In the following three sections, we will discuss the eight disciplines. This is a bit like exploring the individual musical instruments that make up an orchestra. It is important to do, but it also runs the risk of losing sight of the beauty, power, and truth of the whole. I urge you to keep your personal, "nutshell" understanding of the spiritual life in the back of your mind.

## The Disciplines of Training in Wisdom

The Buddha defines wisdom in terms of the mind's horizon, and throughout these readings the word "horizon" is used as a synonym for *wisdom*. When there is little wisdom, the mind's horizon is very constricted. When wisdom is great, the horizon is expansive. One purpose of initially reflecting on the first three truths is to expand the mind's horizon, so that we can better understand the nature of the path, and be more open to it. The danger of taking up the path with too narrow a horizon is that it gets approached simply as a technology for fulfilling egoic desires.

In wisdom, there is a perceptual transformation, which enables a turning away from impermanent Others as sources, or true causes, of happiness and suffering. This turning away is simultaneously a turning toward and into the empty, blissful space of the mind itself. It is perhaps worth noting that there is an interesting use of the "turning" metaphor in Buddhist scripture. When the Buddha turned, in order to see something, he is described as performing "the elephant turn." Apparently, when elephants turn, they turn their entire bodies in the direction of what they want to see, rather than just turning their heads. The commentaries say that all buddhas turn in the same manner. On the one hand, it seems to be a metaphor of congruity; when a buddha turns, he or she *fully* turns. The body is not twisted in different directions by competing agendas. There is full presence of mind in action. So: This turning is the heart of wisdom or spiritual intelligence.

In contrast, spiritual ignorance involves the illusory perception of Others as true sources of happiness and suffering, and the illusory perception of the mind itself as a desolate place of annihilation. This ignorance causes a fearful turning away from the mind itself and a desperate turning toward Others. It is here, in this unwise turning, that desire becomes insatiable, because Others cannot satisfy the longing for the empty, blissful space of the mind itself. Once we see this predicament, we desire to solve it. But solving it is not so easy, because even when we strive to turn in the way of wisdom, the narrowed horizon of illusion only allows us to perceive things in a certain way. We may choose to "turn away" from an Other, but we cannot simply choose to no longer perceive that Other as a true cause of happiness or suffering. We cannot simply choose to no longer perceive the clear space of the mind itself as desolate and threatening. We cannot simply choose to have a broader horizon. In short, egoic consciousness cannot do the sort of turning that is involved in wisdom. It remains preoccupied with the loss of the Other and fear of an Other-free space. The horizon must somehow be expanded.

The teaching of the path begins with an understanding of the importance of the mind's horizon itself, and how it expands when we are following the path and contracts when we are not.

My horizon is everything that it is possible for me to see or experience. It is my most fundamental understanding of life, of the way things are, that frames every aspect of my consciousness. How I think, what I say, my gross level actions, all of my subtle mental processes—all of these get their particular shape and quality and meaning from the horizon. The mind's horizon has an objective grounding (what I can see) called "understanding" and a subjective grounding (how I relate internally to what I can see) called "intention." Both continuously influence and mutually determine one another. Through practicing right under-standing and right intention I seek to broaden this horizon. My wisdom is the breadth of my horizon, and there is always room for it to expand. Intention is a valid and reliable gauge of the accuracy of understanding. If how I relate internally to what I see in my horizon is with reactivity, then what I am seeing in my hori-zon is not what is actually there, not the reality described by the Four Noble Truths.

Right understanding can see the Four Noble Truths manifest, while wrong understanding cannot. Because understanding is conditioned by intention, the relative accuracy of understanding depends on the relative freedom of intention from the reactivities of clinging, aversion, and intentional ignorance. When intention is free, understanding sees in its horizon the truth of the way things are, and the Four Noble Truths manifest.

Because understanding and intention are constantly influenc-ing one another, the mind's horizon cannot be expanded without simultaneously cultivating both its objective and subjective groundings. This problem is one that an ordinary, egoic level of consciousness cannot solve. A solution requires an operation of a much deeper level of mind, one which can make a right effort to understand without clinging or rejecting or ignoring. In such an effort, free of agendas other than to understand, the mind invites the Other to be itself. It extends itself to the Other, relat-ing to it as a "Thou," in a spirit of accepting, respectful interest. It is this mind process that that has the actual capacity to resolve wrong intention. It can make the right effort to understand the reactivities of aversion, clinging, and ignoring, to understand them respectfully as they actually are—as impermanent, decaying "Others" that have arisen in the mind. Under its compassionate, non-intrusive gaze, it gives them the freedom that they require to follow their nature, to live their momentary lifespan—to flower, endure briefly, and to die. And when they have thus been allowed to cease, intention is free. With this greater freedom of intention from reactivity, understanding is more capable of seeing the Other clearly, as it is, without distortion. Intention and understanding have thus simultaneously purified one other, made one another "right."

One way of imagining the process is to envision wrong intention as existing in a superficial region of the mind, where illusion dominates, and right intention as existing in a much deeper region, where there is freedom from illusion. Right intention extends itself from the depths of the pure mind to its cloudy or obscured surface, making wrong intention its object. Through this process, the mind purifies itself of its illusions and their associated reactivities. Right intention is not different than nirodha. Wrong intention is not different than tanha, and thus, until it is resolved, wrong intention leads inevitably to the misery of

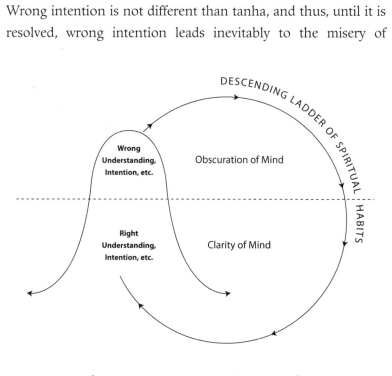

dukkha. The important general principle here is that problems are best solved by understanding and responding to them from a deeper level of consciousness. We see this continually in the sutras, where the Buddha's response to a situation seems to come out of "left field," but ends up being the best solution, because he is responding to the problem from a broader horizon that better understands what is actually happening.

## How Wisdom Training Affects All of Consciousness

Right intention and right understanding affect all of consciousness in the following ways:

- They continually maintain themselves in consciousness by infusing the "will," or inner effort-making.
- They continually notice themselves in relation to the various experiences of the body, the emotions, states of pleasure/pain, and other mental phenomena by infusing attention.
- They continually stay focused on the evolution of personal agency toward greater purity by infusing the mind's capacity for absorption.
- They continually express themselves in communication by suffusing speech.
- They continually express themselves in concrete actions by suffusing bodily movements.
- They continually express themselves in livelihood or vocation by infusing how the mind plans, commits, and occupies time.

So what if, at a particular moment, my mind is full of reactivity, and I am not aware of right understanding and intention? How are these "deep" levels of mind able to reach and transform the reactive surface of the mind that is writhing in illusion? What are the links that connect the mind's reactive surface to its clear, still depths? It is the processes of human agency, beginning with attention, that link the mind's surface to its depths. The three trainings actively cultivate habits in how we attend, how we understand, how we intend, how we judge, how we decide, how we act, how we reflect, and how we remember. These habits facilitate connection between the gross, reactive mind and its still, subtle depths. Together, these habits function like a descending staircase, bringing awareness of one region of the mind to another (cf. diagram, p. 98).

Taking up the three trainings is the practical way to expand the mind's horizon, the practical way to simultaneously cultivate its objective and subjective groundings. The training in wisdom focuses on understanding the mind's horizon itself, through a process of thoughtful study, personal reflection, and cultivating a deeper awareness of the brahma viharas. The training in meditation focuses on how the mind's horizon is reflected and expanded within the interior world of arising thoughts, emotions, bodily experiences, and other mind states. The training in virtue focuses on how the mind's horizon is reflected and expanded within interactive relationships with Others, including oneself.

All habits, whether helpful or harmful, take time and practice to form and strengthen, and it is here that the element of spiritual discipline becomes important. Initially, walking down the path of training has a more awkward quality of self-conscious effort, of striving to do it the "right" way as opposed to the "wrong" way. But gradually, the process becomes more fluid and takes on a self-transcendent quality. This ego transcendence, or insight, occurs on a large scale over a lifetime, but it can also be experienced on a very small scale, such as within a given meditation or reflection period, or in a given moment of interaction with another person, a material object, or some aspect of one's own bodily experience. Right intention is perpetually in motion, seeking to pervade the mind. In cultivating the mental habits that make up the three trainings, we become increasingly aware of right intention. Then, the awareness that one is engaging in the disciplines of training gives way to a deeper awareness of the mind itself, which is more spacious than historical character, and is already virtuous, aware, and wise.

In this way, the three trainings evolve through practice into a unified art of living. The multiple seamless connections between our horizon, our inner life, and our interpersonal life become more intuitively clear, and the path is increasingly experienced as one multi-layered process.

## The Wisdom of Virtue

The virtue disciplines of the path—right speech, action, and livelihood—at the gross level place a strong emphasis on "refraining" from doing harm, rather than an emphasis on "engaging" in doing helpful things. In Buddhist ethics, harmlessness always precedes helpfulness. Ultimately in the Buddha's Dharma, there is no difference between a harmless mind and a loving mind. With the cessation of hating, love naturally flows. With the cessation of egoic consciousness, the pure nature of the mind itself moves into expression. And so, in this approach to ethics, the key is to ensure that meditative awareness and wise reflection are active prior to engaging in gross level actions such as speaking. This approach is in contrast to karmic, ideal-based ethics, which focus primarily on how well gross-level actions conform to a conceptual ideal. From a Buddhist perspective, the karmic approach is far superior to having no concerns regarding harmfulness and helpfulness, but still inferior to an awareness-based ethic. In the process of training in virtue, we inevitably engage in a mixture of karmic, ideal-based practice and awareness-based practice. The training encourages evolution in the direction of decreasing suffering through increasing awareness-based living.

In virtue training, we learn to not prematurely engage in gross level actions that we consider helpful, without exploring the subtle levels of our experience as best we can. Otherwise, we run the risk of acting in ways that are incongruent with our actual understandings, intentions, and inner experience. When this happens, it generates confusion and suffering, both for ourselves and for those around us. And so, for example, our practice of right speech at the gross level begins simply with refraining from harmful communications, and then moves into awareness of our inner experience. As right intentions are realized, there is speaking, or refraining from speaking, in ways that are actively helpful. This process may seem cumbersome at first, because it usually involves a significant lifestyle change. It assumes a level of ongoing engagement in meditative awareness and wise reflection outside of formal practice periods.

Of course, virtue training is not only about refraining from harm. It also involves the active cultivation of interpersonal goodwill, helpfulness, sensitivity, generosity, honesty, and temperance in one's attitudes and concrete actions toward others. It is just that virtuous action is not simply a matter of acting or thinking according to certain positive ideals. Wholesome attitudes, to be sustained, need to be well rooted in and nourished by a peaceful mind. Such a mind can be discovered, awareness of it can be deepened, but it cannot be manufactured.

Training in virtue is perhaps the most misunderstood and neglected practice in Western Buddhism. Its role in the path as a whole is not well appreciated. One purpose of virtue training is to strengthen helpful patterns of character (skillfulness). While these habit patterns themselves are not virtue, they can facilitate virtue training. By cultivating character development in certain directions, you are also influencing the habitual thoughts that will arise in the various phases of the process of personal agency—and this can make everyday life much easier.

What does it mean, then, to "practice" the path? It means to recognize it and to follow it as it moves through the ordinary processes of being human. Through the three trainings, character learns what is worth remembering in life and what is not. It learns what leads to the cessation of suffering and what does not. Through training, character becomes a context for recognizing the movement of the path within us. Character, for better or

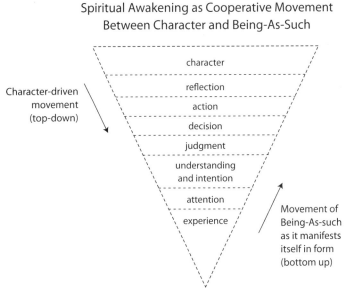

Spiritual Awakening as Cooperative Movement
Between Character and Being-As-Such

Character-driven movement (top-down)

character
reflection
action
decision
judgment
understanding and intention
attention
experience

Movement of Being-As-such as it manifests itself in form (bottom up)

Being-As-Such

worse, always functions as a kind of coach for attention, under-standing, intention, judgment, decision, action, reflection, and remembering. But within the three trainings, that coaching becomes consciously focused on the recognition of one's true nature. We can think of spiritual awakening as a process in which there is an increasingly cooperative movement between character and Being-As-Such. As we train, as we follow the path, we increasingly understand what that means.

As we engage in the trainings of the path, there really is no way to avoid the development of experiential insight into the tran-scendental dimension of who we are. At the transcendent level of awareness, the path is personal agency being consciously infused by Being-As-Such. At the karmic level of awareness, agency is thought to originate in an autonomous self. But the path oper-ates at both of these levels in the training process, and as practice progresses, it moves more deeply into the transcendent level. When, in the lives of his disciples, practice wasn't progressing in this direction, when the disciples would get "stuck" at a karmic level of practice, the Buddha would counsel them to attend more, or perhaps less, to one area of practice or another. Such counsel and encouragement is important, because the karmic level of practice, like samsara in general, can be an enticing "weigh sta-tion"; it can tempt us to forget that we are on a journey and dis-engage from training. Without an increasing awareness of the subtle presence of Being-As-Such in our lives, character easily becomes consumed by the spell of its own stories.

# CHAPTER TEN

# The Disciplines of Training in Virtue

The three disciplines of virtue training are (1) right speech, (2) right action, and (3) right livelihood. Each of these disciplines involves processes at the gross, subtle, and very subtle levels of consciousness.

## The Discipline of Right Speech

The power of self-expression to both help and harm is the focus of the discipline of right speech. This power is contained not just in the semantic contents of words, but also in the use of silence, gesture, facial expression, timing, and the more subtle implications of the context and emotional tone in which words are spoken. These more subtle aspects of the art of self-expression often reveal core understandings and intentions as much as, if not more than, words themselves.

At the gross level of character and action, the discipline of right speech involves

+ first refraining from communications that foster the impoverishment of basic physical and social well-being; refraining from communications that are abusive, coercive, malicious, manipulative, empty, deceitful, gossipy, or otherwise not helpful;

- then moving on to explore communication at the subtle level of inner experience.

At the subtle level of interior life, the discipline of right speech involves

- becoming aware of wrong intentions such as the intention to lie or use speech to conceal one's actual harmful intentions; the intention to gossip, speak maliciously or coercively; and the intention to speak useless, meaningless, or empty words. This involves
  - Noticing the spreading of these wrong intentions into thoughts, bodily reactions, emotions, and other states of mind;
  - Making internal efforts to weaken these wrong intentions by not becoming mentally absorbed in them or related thoughts or emotions, and attending to them in a way that allows them to naturally fade.
- becoming aware of right intentions, such as the intention to speak the truth in a way that is beneficial and timely; the intention to express friendliness; the intention to express joy over another's well-being; the intention to express compassion; and the intention to express the desire to understand. This involves
  - noticing the spreading of these right intentions into thoughts, bodily reactions, emotions, and other states of mind;
  - making internal efforts to strengthen these right intentions, becoming mentally absorbed in them and related thoughts, emotions, etc.
- moving on to explore the very subtle level of mind.

At the very subtle level of the mind, the practice of right speech involves

- reflecting on what is presently being experienced in the communication situation, in terms of who it is that wants to speak or to remain silent. If that one is discovered to be the ego, its hold on consciousness is then dissolved through developing insight into its true nature. This involves reflecting on the communication process in terms of the first three truths:
    - identifying the unique misery of dukkha;
    - recognizing the fantasy of tanha;
    - and, in the wake of tanha's dissolution, experiencing the expanded consciousness of nirodha in the context of communication.

## Right Action

The focus of this discipline is the power of bodily actions to both help and harm.

At the gross level of character and action, the discipline of right action involves

- first refraining from actions that foster the impoverishment of the basic physical and social well-being of self and others, and also bodily actions such as killing, harming, stealing, sexually exploiting, and becoming intoxicated (or otherwise unaware of the impact of one's actions);
- then moving on to explore action at the subtle level of inner experience.

At the subtle level of interior life, the practice of right action involves

- becoming aware of tainted intentions such as the intention to harm; the intention to steal; the intention to deceive; the intention to emotionally or sexually exploit; the intention to become intoxicated. This involves
  - noticing the spreading of these tainted intentions into thoughts, bodily reactions, emotions, and other states of mind;
  - making internal efforts to weaken these tainted intentions by not becoming mentally absorbed in them or related thoughts or emotions, and attending to them in a way that allows them to naturally fade.
- becoming aware of right intentions such as the intention to help; the intention to give what is needed; the intention to respect emotional and sexual boundaries; and the intention to protect our awareness of the impact of our actions. This involves
  - noticing the spreading of these right intentions into thoughts, bodily reactions, emotions, and other states of mind;
  - making internal efforts to strengthen these right intentions and become mentally absorbed in them and related thoughts, emotions, etc.
- moving on to explore the very subtle level of consciousness.

At the very subtle level of the mind, the practice of right action involves

- reflecting on what is presently being experienced at the subtle level of consciousness, in terms of who it is that wants to act or refrain from acting. If that one is discovered to be the ego, its hold on consciousness is then dissolved through developing insight into its true nature. This involves reflecting on the process of bodily action in terms of the first three truths:

- o identifying the unique misery of dukkha;
- o recognizing the fantasy of tanha;
- o and, in the wake of tanha's dissolution, experiencing the expanded consciousness of nirodha within the domain of physical action.

## *Right Livelihood*

Right livelihood includes the disciplines of both right speech and right action, but focuses on their manifestation in the broader context of the commitments that we make that occupy our time. If we currently work for a living, that commitment likely takes up a large portion of our time. But any regular time-consuming commitment is the focus of this discipline.

At the gross level of character and action, the practice of right livelihood involves

- first refraining from commitments that occupy our time in ways that interfere with our spiritual development: commitments that facilitate or require the impoverishment of the basic physical and social well-being of self or others, wrong speech, or wrong actions (see above);
- then moving on to explore livelihood/vocation at the subtle level of inner experience.

At the subtle level of interior life, the practice of right livelihood involves

- becoming aware of wrong intentions such as the intention to commit our time in ways that would involve

wrong speech, wrong actions, or other such intentions
that would interfere with our spiritual development:

- ○ noticing the spreading of these wrong intentions into
  thoughts, plans, bodily reactions, emotions, and
  other states of mind;
- ○ making internal efforts to weaken these wrong intentions by not becoming mentally absorbed in them or
  related thoughts, plans, emotions, etc., and attending
  to them in a way that allows them to naturally fade.

- ◆ becoming aware of right intentions, such as the intention to commit our time in ways that foster our spiritual
  development and are beneficial for others:
  - ○ noticing the spreading of these right intentions into
    thoughts, plans, bodily reactions, emotions, and
    other states of mind;
  - ○ making internal efforts to strengthen these right
    intentions, becoming mentally absorbed in them and
    related thoughts, emotions, etc.

- ◆ moving on to explore the very subtle level of consciousness.

At the very subtle level of the mind, the practice of right livelihood involves

- ◆ reflecting on what is presently being experienced at the
  subtle level of consciousness, in terms of who it is that
  wants to commit or not commit to certain ways of
  spending time. If that one is discovered to be the ego, its
  hold on consciousness is then dissolved through developing insight into its true nature. This involves reflecting on the process of vocational commitment in terms
  of the first three truths:
  - ○ identifying the unique misery of dukkha;

- recognizing the fantasy of tanha;
- and, in the wake of tanha's dissolution, experiencing the expanded consciousness of nirodha in the context of vocation.

# CHAPTER ELEVEN

# The Disciplines of Training in Meditative Awareness

The three disciplines of training in meditative awareness are (1) right effort, (2) right mindfulness, or attention, and (3) right absorption. Though identified primarily with meditation, training in meditative awareness extends far beyond formal meditation practices to how we subjectively experience ourselves at any time. Like the trainings in virtue, each of these three disciplines involves processes at the gross, subtle, and very subtle levels of consciousness.

## Right Effort

The inner effort involved in this discipline might be called "will." Most Buddhist translators avoid that term, perhaps because it has so many additional complex meanings and associations in Western philosophy, religion, and culture. The simpler word "effort," or "inner effort," may thus be a better choice.

At the gross level of character and action, the discipline of right effort is the impetus behind the overt actions that are involved in

- caring for the needs of the body and reaching out to locate and engage in spiritual community;
- the disciplines of right speech, right action, and right livelihood;
- the setting up and maintaining of regular practices of meditation, study, and reflection.

At the subtle level of interior life, the discipline of right effort is the effort to understand, which involves

- weakening the wrong intentions that have already arisen in the mind, and enabling the arising of right intentions. Wrong intentions refer to the intentions to cling to, reject, escape, destroy, or ignore a given Other that has arisen in the mind. At a slightly more subtle level, they also refer to mental dullness, obsessive worrying, restlessness, and doubting, in which the mental Other is not always apparent. Right intentions refer to intentions to understand a given mental Other on its own terms, relating to it as a *Thou*, allowing it to arise and pass away without any interference.

At the very subtle level of the mind, the practice of right effort involves

- the weakening of very subtle wrong intentions, such as
  - clinging to the ego—clinging to a compelling fantasy that an impermanent, decaying image or view in the mind is one's self, or a part of one's self, or something that belongs to one's self—this prevents the image from experiencing its natural process of fading out of existence;
  - clinging to an object of the ego's desire—clinging to a compelling fantasy that some Other in the mind has the power to liberate the ego, to end its suffering

and usher in its happiness; or clinging to a fantasy that some Other in the mind has the power to destroy the ego, cause its suffering, and prevent its happiness; or clinging to a fantasy that some Other in the mind has the power to distract the ego from Others that really matter;

○ subtle aversion or resistance to reflection on the Four Noble Truths in some particular context.

• the strengthening of very subtle right intentions, such as
  ○ the brahma viharas;
  ○ the desire to remain in the crucible of the present moment;
  ○ the desire to surrender to the pure consciousness of nirodha;
  ○ the desire to be free of egoic consciousness;
  ○ the desire to understand the true nature of one's experience.

• the turning away from barren, impermanent Others, which were once perceived as life-giving and eternal, and turning toward Being-As-Such: the clear, empty, blissful space of the mind itself, which was once perceived as a desolate place of annihilation. This turning of awareness illustrates how wisdom (right understanding and right intention) is infusing right effort. In contrast, the turning toward Others and away from the emptiness of Being-As-Such (wrong effort) illustrates the root illusion that causes suffering. When there is insufficient infusion of effort with wisdom, there may indeed be an attempt to turn away from Others, but the Others are still perceived as life-giving, and emptiness is still perceived as desolate without the Others, and, as a result, the effort provokes anxiety. In that case, there has been no actual turning away from illusion and into the reality of the way things are.

## Right Attention or Right Mindfulness

The Pali word translated here as "mindfulness" or "attention" is *sati*. Sati is a purposeful alertness, which notices what is present and what is not present. When infused with right understanding and right intention, it not only notices, it notices with a kind, respectful, non-intrusive quality that perceives the actual nature of what it sees. It is at that infused level that it becomes right attention. Wrong attention, on the other hand, also notices what is present and what is not present, but all within the frame of reference of the ego. It thus notices all phenomena as either Others the ego wants to possess, Others the ego wants to eliminate or escape from, or Others the ego wants to ignore.

At the gross level of character and action, the discipline of right attention involves purposely noticing

- basic physical and social well-being, or needs, when they are present and when they are not present;
- right speech and right actions, when they are present;
- wrong speech and wrong actions, when they are present.

At the subtle level of interior experience, the discipline of right attention involves

- purposely noticing the various Others that are continually arising and passing away in the stream of consciousness, from moment to moment—this includes bodily sensations, sounds, sights, odors, tastes, thoughts, narratives, mental images, moods, emotions, states of identification with ego, experiences of clinging, averting, or ignoring Others, and any other phenomena that may be experienced in the mind;

• noticing these various Others in a way that is kind, respectful of their separateness, and which does not seek to influence them in any way. Noticing how the presence of right understanding, right intention, right effort, and right absorption infuse and affect the quality of attention, with respect to these various Others;

• noticing the arising of wrong attention with respect to these various Others, which seeks to prolong, eliminate, or ignore their presence—noticing how the presence of wrong understanding, wrong intention, wrong effort, and wrong absorption infuse and affect the quality of attention, with respect to these various Others.

At the very subtle level of the mind, the discipline of right attention involves

• noticing the characteristics of the experience of suffering, in relation to these various Others;

• noticing the characteristics of the experience of egoic fantasies and desires (tanha) in relation to these various Others;

• noticing the characteristics of the cessation of egoic fantasies and desires (nirodha), in relation to these various Others;

• noticing the characteristics of the mind itself (nirodha), apart from these various Others.

## Right Absorption

The Pali word translated here as absorption is *samadhi*. It describes the fullness of the mind's presence to its object (the

Other). In right absorption, all mental energy is dedicated to understanding the Other as it is. It is a kind of abandonment or surrender to understanding the Other, in which no mental energy is withheld in order to evaluate, analyze, compare, elaborate, or concentrate on the meaning of the Other in relation to something else (such as the ego or any other Other). In this sense right absorption is singular or one-pointed, rather than diffuse. It is fully conscious and lucid, however, like a flame, and not a dream-like kind of trance state. Infused with right intention, it is also friendly and accepting. The classic example of wrong absorption, on the other hand, is the way in which a predator stalks its prey. In this case, greed and hatred infuse the absorption, and the Other is understood only as that which the predator desires to possess and/or destroy in order to relieve itself of some tension, which it experiences as dukkha. Much of what are commonly called dynamics of mental illness involve wrong absorption at the subtle level of mind, in which this predator/prey dynamic wreaks havoc out of sight, in the inner life. Much of what is commonly called romance has the same roots, but the havoc that romance wreaks is usually more pleasant and benign.

At the gross level of character and action, the discipline of right absorption involves

- being fully present within acts of caring for basic physical and social needs;
- being fully present within acts of right speech, right action, and right vocation.

At the subtle level of interior experience, the discipline of right absorption involves:

- being fully present to the experience of the brahma viharas.

- being fully present to the particular object (Other) of meditation, such as
  - the sensation of the breath, in tranquility meditation;
  - whatever thought, desire, bodily sensation, or other mental phenomena is currently arising, in insight meditation.
- being fully present to the unstructured, non-physical, space-like medium of the mind itself, within which all of these objects (Others) are arising and passing away.

At the very subtle level of the mind, the discipline of right absorption involves

- being fully present to the experience of the truth of dukkha, as it unfolds in the present moment.
- being fully present to the experience of the truth of tanha, as it unfolds in the present moment.
- being fully present to the experience of the truth of nirodha, as it unfolds in the present moment.
- being fully present to the experience of the truth of magga, the path, as it unfolds in the present moment.

# CHAPTER TWELVE

# Conditioned and Unconditioned Levels of the Path

How we experience the path depends on how we experience ourselves. At those moments when we are convinced that our personality (or some idealized one) is the living essence of who we are, we experience the "conditioned," "mundane," or "karmic" level of the path. The karmic level of the path builds and affirms one's identity as a skillful agent. At those moments when we experience nirodha, we experience the "unconditioned," "supramundane," or "transcendent" level of the path. The transcendent level of the path operates below the mythic level of samsara, where the "skillful agent" is revealed to be only a useful fiction that helps us to make sense of, and feel in control of, what is actually a much more complex and mysterious process. The summary chart below attempts to describe in words how these different levels of the path might feel in actual experience, as one moves back and forth on the path between different levels of consciousness. It is not meant to guide practice, only to give a sense of how differently identity can be experienced and how this difference affects our perception of the path. Outwardly, these inner differences might appear very similar.

As we follow the path, we are always either accruing positive karma by constructing a better—more flexible, sensitive, and ethically oriented—character, which we still imagine to be our essential self, or we are moving out of that illusion about who we are,

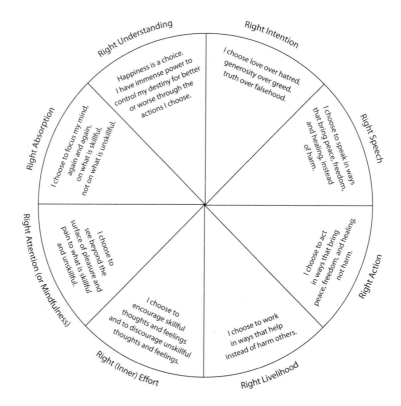

*How a conditioned path experience might feel*

and into the wise and virtuous bliss of nirodha. And so, a funny thing happens on the way to nirvana: by the time we reach that level of development, we have already enjoyed a fascinating spiritual journey, and built a beautiful, virtuous, and useful character, which we are finally able to fully let go of, because there are no longer any doubts about our true identity.

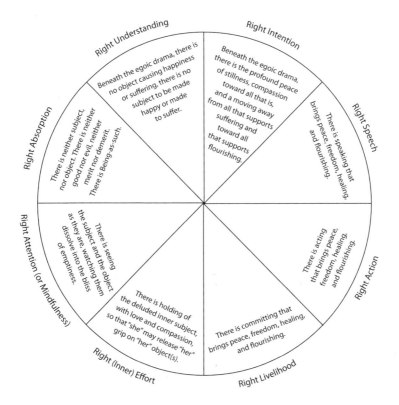

*How an unconditioned path experience might feel*

# CHAPTER THIRTEEN

# Taking Spiritual Refuge—A Ritual of Commitment to the Path

## *The General Meaning of Taking Spiritual Refuge*

There are many possible modes of existence—we can meditate, paint, pray, play games, spend time with friends, sing, write poetry, fight crime and oppression, do physical exercise, earn money, take naps, wash clothes, vote, raise children, appreciate nature, listen to music, and on and on and on. The possibilities are endless. We realize through living, however, that we cannot live all of these modes at the same time and with the same intensity. We have to make choices.

Psychologist Adrian van Kaam suggests that a key existential choice that we make in life is the choice of what our *central mode of existence* will be. Every person has a central mode of existence, even though it is seldom chosen in a conscious way. With the choice of a central mode of existence, other modes of existence immediately become, naturally, peripheral. By consciously or unconsciously choosing one's central mode of existence, the peripheral modes are placed in a subordinate relation to that central mode. The peripheral modes then derive their shape, color, and meaning from that central mode. Then, when there is freedom to act, peripheral modes of being are fostered only as they nourish and do not draw one away from the central reality of his or her life. This natural hierarchy also gives the person a foundation for making other choices. It illumines criteria for saying "yes," "no," or "maybe" to the many possible subordinate modes of existence, and as well answers questions regarding how to and why to embody them.

Through a ritual of spiritual refuge a person affirms the intention to establish a particular central mode of existence in his or her life. It is undertaken when, after a period of self-exploration, study, experimentation, and reflection on the meaning of life, a person understands and feels that the best possible central mode, or heart, of his or her existence is spiritual in nature. Although thinking is involved in this process, the decision to make this choice is not reached through an abstract thought process but through dialogue and personal insights, which are rooted in experience.

Spiritual refuge only has meaning in the context of spiritual vulnerability. Taking refuge thus requires some awareness and insight concerning this vulnerability in one's own experience. In terms of refuge, our primary spiritual vulnerability is the vulnerability to let our lives be unconsciously defined and lived out as a samsaric fantasy. To realize this is to realize that our central mode of existence is frequently not conscious but reflexive. It is to realize that our well-being erodes when we simply go with this reflexive flow of life. It is to realize that our well-being and the well-being of others are deeply connected to our central mode of existence. Others benefit from our well-being, and we benefit from theirs, in ways that cannot always be explained.

Spiritual refuge is a great undertaking, but, at the same time, it is only a humble beginning. Rather than being a once-and-for-all transformation, it is more like the formal planting of a seed that, in order to grow, will need to be cared for and cultivated, in good times and bad, for the remainder of one's life. It is a formal entry, and recognition of that entry, into a spiritual way of living, as understood by whatever wisdom tradition one follows. It is a recognition that, to some extent, the heart has already made this commitment, just as the union in a marriage often begins long before the ritual ceremony.

In the Buddhist tradition, making the existential choice that the central mode of existence in one's life is spiritual in nature is expressed as taking refuge in the "Triple Gem" of the Buddha, the Dharma, and the Sangha. Taking refuge in the Triple Gem is paradoxically a ritual of initiation in the Buddhist tradition and also the most advanced of all Buddhist practices. This is because these words—Buddha, Dharma, and Sangha—not only summarize the Buddhist way of life, but are also symbols that point to the ultimate nature of reality itself. Because of this, their "complete meaning" only comes through spiritual insight and is impossible to disclose in words. Their practical meaning, however, can be expressed in words:

*The Buddha.* Through a process of practice and reflection, the person who engages in the refuge ritual is coming to understand that the mind itself already contains and always contained all that is needed in life, not in terms of factual information or acquired skills, but in terms of its very nature. This inspires a desire to take refuge, to dwell within the safe harbors of this subtle level of mind, symbolized by the word Buddha, which means "The One Who Is Awake."

*The Dharma.* Further, the person who engages in the refuge ritual is coming to understand that life itself has a primordial structure, which is articulated, as much as is possible in words, in the Four Noble Truths of dukkha, tanha, nirodha, and magga—truths that have been realized by the wise in all times and places. This inspires a desire to take refuge within this primordial wisdom, symbolized by the word "dharma," which in this case means both "the teachings of the wise" and "the truth of the way things are."

***The Sangha.*** The person who engages in the refuge ritual is also coming to understand that these symbols of the Buddha and the Dharma have not arisen in his or her consciousness apart from the good intentions and efforts of countless human beings who, from time immemorial, in the living of their lives considered the potential influence that their actions could have on others. Those beings are the Sangha, which means "community." This inspires a desire to take refuge, to become a part of that lineage, and to consciously participate in its community.

For one who follows the way of the Buddha, to live is to continually take refuge in the Triple Gem within the myriad of his or her experiences between birth and death. Life is consecrated to that purpose. Taking refuge is not a doctrinal or creedal commitment. It does not involve holding any particular beliefs "no matter what." Instead, it is an *existential* commitment, which means that it is only made and sustained based on evidence of its value that is derived from one's own existence. As a result of taking refuge and its trainings, a person should notice clear improvements in his or her attention, understandings, judgments, decisions, actions, reflections, and character. And the criterion of clear improvement is movement out of suffering and into flourishing, both in our own lives and the lives of those who are affected by our actions. Thus, the basis of our commitment to the path is not an authority outside of our own existence. Neither is it absolutely individualistic. This is explained by the Buddha in a famous discourse to a community called the Kalamas, who were plagued with religious doubts:

> Don't go by testimonies, by legends, by traditions, by scripture, by logical conjecture, by inference, by analogies, by agreement through pondering views, by probability, or by the thought, "This contemplative is our teacher, so we should follow." Only when you know for yourselves that, "These practices are beneficial; these practices are blameless; these practices are praised by those who are clearly wise; these practices, when adopted and carried out, lead to evident welfare and to happiness"—only then do you have a valid reason to enter and remain in them.

## Spiritual Vocation and the Politics of Awakening

A liberating understanding of the Buddha's Four Noble Truths manifests socially and politically in a way of being with others that is different in quality from samsara's dynamics of dominance and submission. The sociopolitical agenda of the Four Noble Truths, if I can call it that, is very clearly to create a culture of compassion, where all beings are protected from harm and nurtured toward spiritual awakening. This is, however, an organic agenda. It is a shared interest in and commitment to ways of living that create a compassionate culture. In the Buddhist tradition this spiritual vocation is described as the way of the bodhisattva. The way of the bodhisattva is a natural development in minds that are growing more and more accustomed to the transcendental peace encountered in momentary cessations of craving and aversion. Such minds grow increasingly aware of their basic interrelatedness with all living beings, and increasingly experienced in the unobstructed flow of Being-As-Such through the processes of personal agency. The bodhisattva way is a wholesome passion that arises in a mind that is coming to know its true, boundless nature through Dharma training. Bodhisattvas share the insight that their lives of virtue, meditative awareness, and wisdom constitute real benefits that are freely offered to the world, just as they themselves have benefited from the lives of bodhisattvas who came before them. They experience their lives as belonging to this compassionate lineage. In its doctrine of the bodhisattva way, Buddhist spirituality follows the lead of the historical Buddha and participates in the development of an organized community of like-minded persons who act consciously, wisely, and virtuously for the benefit of all sentient beings.

The Buddhist understanding of the common good and how best to foster it is thus very complex, involving multiple levels of reality and consciousness. It reveres the bodhisattva as the true "politician," the one whose actions truly benefit the common life of the *polis*, or community. In our contemporary culture, the word "politics" has unfortunately come to mean inept, malevolent, or otherwise reactionary politics, which arise more from egocentricity and its collective variants than from wise and compassionate concern for the common good. In contrast, a bodhisattva is not a reactionary. He or she understands that beneficial actions arise from a mind that is purifying itself from influences such as greed and hatred. He or she understands the validity of a given social action in terms of the validity of the mind from which the action arises. What matters most, in terms of the ultimate benefit of an action, are the clarity and intentionality of the mind enacting it, not the outer form of the action alone. This includes "political" actions, those actions that are allegedly performed on behalf of others, for their common good. Politics has everything to do with spirituality, because political actions only arise out of human agency, out of particular ways of attending, understanding, intending, judging, and deciding with respect to particular experiences. Thus, from a Buddhist perspective, engagement in the three trainings of the path is essential for sound social and political action.

As we pursue training in virtue, meditative awareness, and wisdom, we gradually unlearn the basics of the samsaric illusions in which our lives get stuck. Remarkably, in this experience of unlearning, the Buddha's path to recovery and happiness rises to meet us within our own mind. It is as though, once the noise of egoic consciousness quiets down sufficiently, we begin to hear the more subtle voice of the Buddha, compassionately revealing to us the basics of a new life. At the beginning of our training, we might have regarded such an inner voice as a figment of the imagination. But over time, as we experience increasing liberation from samsara's illusions, we develop a deeper understanding of what is real and what is beneficial. We realize that unlearning the basics has only been a gateway into hearing the voice of this great inner sage, who has so very much to teach us about ourselves and life.

Still, the Four Noble Truths, on which this primer of Buddhist spirituality is based, remain an object for a lifetime of reflection. Experiential training is the key to understanding them. Experiential training simply means learning *in vivo*—in your own life—the processes of practicing virtue, meditation, and wisdom.

May you always know the inconceivably great blessings of the Buddha, the Dharma, and the Sangha in your life's journey.

# Index

chitta, 2. *See also* mind

Christianity, xvi, 14, 19

clinging, 30, 31, 97, 114. *See
    also* grasping
    Silent Watcher and, 78
    spiritual path and, 65

coherence, sense of, 45

compass metaphor, 14

compassion, 20, 67, 77, 97,
    130–31
    nirodha and, 49
    sangha and, 11
    virtue training and, 106

congruity, metaphor of, 95

consciousness
    dependent origination and,
        72–76
    eight dimensions of the
        path and, 89, 91–92
    levels of, 5–7, 121–23
    love and, 17, 19
    mature spirituality and, 55,
        56
    nirodha and, 45–47, 50, 52
    obscurations and, 7–12
    Silent Watcher and, 76–78
    taking refuge and, 128–29
    tanha and, 36–41
    virtue training and, 108–10
    wholistic, 2–5

wisdom training and, 99,
    101

contemplative living, xvi, 12–14

crucible, spiritual path as, 90–
    92

**D**

death, 22, 26, 98

decision, role of, 67–68

defilements. *See* obscurations

delusion, 7–12. *See also* illusion

dependent origination, 63, 71–
    76

desire, 19, 21, 53, 95, 114, 117.
    *See also* tanha (thirst)

Dhammacakkapavatana Sutta
    (Turning the Wheel of
    Dharma), x

Dhammapada, 7

Dharma, 64, 93–94, 101. *See
    also* dharmas
    in the Dhammapada, 7
    nirodha and, 46, 47–48, 52
    obscurations and, 10, 8–12
    reflection and, 69
    spiritual discipline and, 80,
        84, 86
    taking refuge and, 127–28,
        130, 131
    tanha and, 39
    use of the term, xiii

emptiness (shunyata), 58, 61, 115, 123
equality, 53
equanimity, 77
ethics, 101, 102. *See also* morality
evil, 38
existence, mode of, choosing one's central, 125–26
existential choices, 125–26, 128
existentialism, 14
experience, pure, 64, 72, 75, 78, 91
experiential training, 131

**F**
fantasy, 107, 109, 111, 115
   flight from pain into, 23–41
   nirodha and, 49, 53
fear, 30, 53, 77
Four Noble Truths, ix–x, 22–41, 67, 80
   Being-As-Such and, 61
   eight dimensions of the path and, 92
   lokadharma and, 22
   meditative awareness and, 115
   overview of, xiii–xvi

right understanding and, 87–90
taking refuge and, 128, 129, 131
wisdom training and, 97

**G**
generosity, 8, 94, 102
God, 16
goodwill, need for, 20
grandiosity, 30
grasping, 34, 48. *See also* clinging
greed, 8, 20, 29, 39, 77
gurus, 30

**H**
harmony, 21
hatred, 8, 20, 39, 77
health issues, 9, 11, 39
heart, 77, 86
   that holds the whole world, 6
   contemplative living and, 13
   use of the term, 2–3
   of wisdom, 95
home
   flourishing at, 43–54
   location of, 45–47
hope, 53, 86

mammals, 16. *See also* animals
meditation, 59, 100–102
    action and, 68
    awareness of, training in,
        113–19, 131
    eight dimensions of the
        path and, 89, 90
    formal, 52
    groups, 11
    levels of consciousness
        and, 6
    Silent Watcher and, 67,
        71–76
    spiritual discipline and, 81,
        82
    wisdom and, 93–94
mental objects, 36
metaphysics, x, 6, 13, 37
metta, 18
Middle Way, 55–61, 65, 90
mind
    attention and, 64
    clarity of, five necessities
        for the development of,
        9–10
    eight dimensions of the
        path and, 89, 91–92
    large/small, in the Tibetan
        tradition, 64
    levels of consciousness
        and, 5–7

love and, 17, 19
meditative awareness and,
    115, 117–19
natural state of, 8–9
nirodha and, 44, 46–47,
    49–52
obscurations and, 8–12
tanha and, 32–33
true nature of, 46–47, 54
views of, 1–5
virtue training and, 106–7,
    110
wisdom and, 95–99, 100
mindfulness, 64, 87–92, 116–
    17, 122–23
mode of existence, choosing
    one's central, 125–26
morality, 37. *See also* ethics
muditha, 18
Muslim tradition, xvi, 14
mutuality, 53

**N**
nirodha (cessation), xv, 43–54,
    56–57
    eclipse of, 48–51
    eight dimensions of the
        path and, 87, 92
    levels of the path and, 123
    meditative awareness and,
        115, 117, 119

path from, to nirvana, 51–
54
right intention and, 98
taking refuge and, 128
virtue training and, 107,
109, 111
nirvana, path from nirodha to,
51–54
Nishida, Kitaro, 72

**O**
objectivity, 62, 97, 100
obscurations, 7–12, 75
ontology, x
Ottawa, 59

**P**
pain
dependent origination and,
72
flight from, into fantasy,
23–41
lokadharma and, 21
nirodha and, 47
parents, 15–16, 21–22, 45
path. *See* spiritual path
patience, 30, 37, 84
peace, 11, 30, 33
inner, as outer peace, 79–80
politics of awakening and,
129–30

politics, of awakening, 129–31
positive thinking, 7
Protestant tradition, xvi. *See
also* Christianity
psychology, xiv, 18, 19, 83
Silent Watcher and, 78
tanha and, 31, 32–33, 35
pure experience, 64, 72, 75,
78, 91
purification, 91–92

**R**
reactivity, 98, 100
reflection, 68–69
refuge, taking, 125–31
relationships, cultivation of,
53–54. *See also* sangha;
spiritual community
reptiles, 16
resistance
wise, 84–86
working with, 83–84
right absorption, 64, 87–92,
117–19, 122–23
right action, 87–92, 101–4,
107–9, 114, 122–23
right attention, 116–17
right effort, 64, 87–92, 113–16,
122–23
right intention, 78, 83, 87–
93, 96–98, 99–101,

# About the Author

Dr. Rishi Sativihari was born Richard Wright and grew up in the inner city of Detroit during the 1960s and 70s. Prior to monastic life, Rishi worked as the clinical director of La Casa, a drug abuse treatment center in southwest Detroit, and as a staff psychologist for the University of Toronto, Department of Psychiatry. Rishi received his monastic training and ordination from the Venerable Wattegama Dhammawasa at the Subodharama Monastery in Sri Lanka. He also trained in the Tibetan (Gelug) tradition under the Venerable Geshe Tashi Tsering at the Chenrezig Monastery in Australia, and under S.N. Goenka at the Dhammagiri Centre in India. In 2003, Rishi left monastic life and began training in the contemplative foundations of Judaism and Christianity at the Toronto School of Theology. He currently offers teaching on contemplative living and guidance in spiritual formation to individuals and groups in the Toronto area.

✳

---

# About Wisdom Publications

Wisdom Publications, a nonprofit publisher, is dedicated to making available authentic works relating to Buddhism for the benefit of all. We publish books by ancient and modern masters in all traditions of Buddhism, translations of important texts, and original scholarship. Additionally, we offer books that explore East-West themes unfolding as traditional Buddhism encounters our modern culture in all its aspects. Our titles are published with the appreciation of Buddhism as a living philosophy, and with the special commitment to preserve and transmit important works from Buddhism's many traditions.

To learn more about Wisdom, or to browse books online, visit our website at www.wisdompubs.org.

You may request a copy of our catalog online or by writing to this address:

Wisdom Publications
199 Elm Street
Somerville, Massachusetts 02144 USA
Telephone: 617-776-7416
Fax: 617-776-7841
Email: info@wisdompubs.org
www.wisdompubs.org